THE BOOK OF CROSS STITCH

AN ESSENTIAL GUIDE

MATERIALS, TOOLS AND EQUIPMENT, READING THE CHART, THE STITCHES

INCLUDES 39 CROSS STITCH PROJECTS

DURENE JONES

Tuva Publishing
www.tuvapublishing.com

Address Merkez Mah. Cavusbasi Cad. No71
Cekmekoy - Istanbul 34782 Turkey
Tel +90 216 642 62 62

The Book of Cross Stitch an Essential Guide

First Print 2023 / February

All Global Copyrights Belong To
Tuva Tekstil ve Yayıncılık Ltd.

Content Cross Stitch

Editor in Chief Ayhan DEMİRPEHLİVAN
Project Editor Kader DEMİRPEHLİVAN
Author Durene JONES
Technical Editors Leyla ARAS
Graphic Designers Ömer ALP, Abdullah BAYRAKÇI,
Tarık TOKGÖZ, Yunus GÜLDOĞAN
Photography Tuva Publishing

ISBN 978-605-7834-53-9

CONTENTS

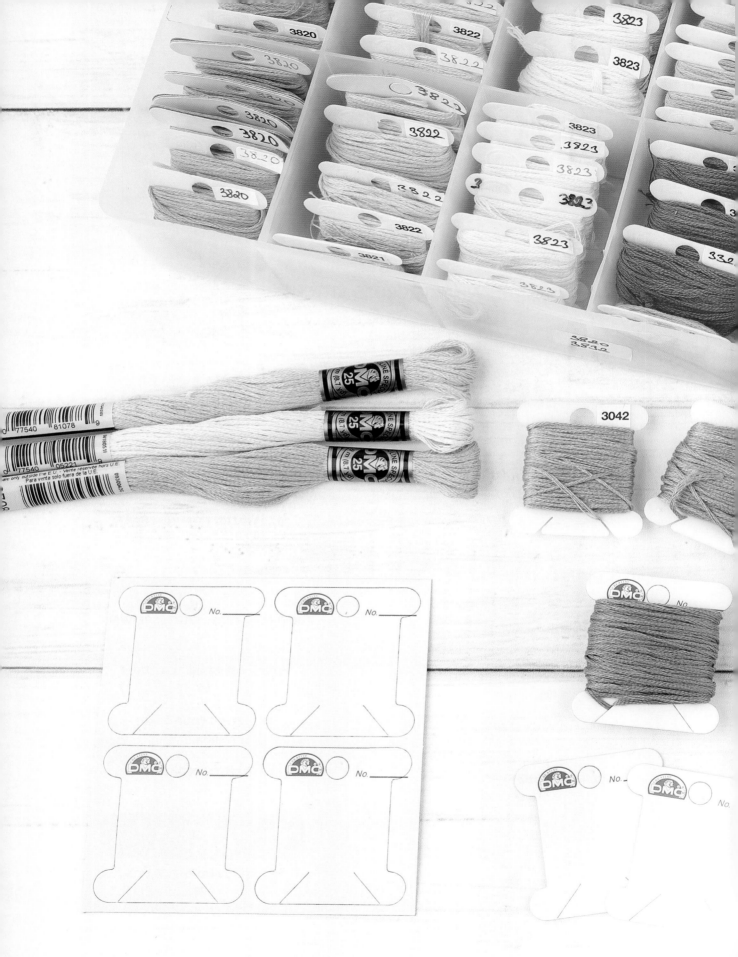

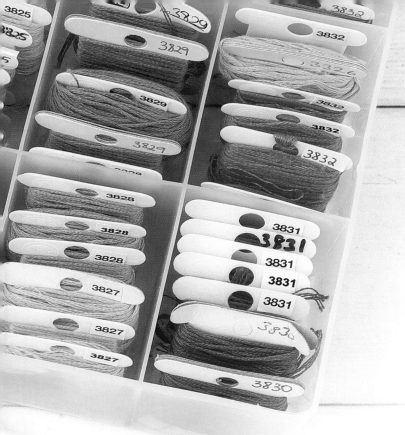

INTRODUCTION

Cross stitch is one of the oldest and simplest forms of embroidery stitches, and can be seen in the heritage of many countries around the world, although the style of the designs may change, the basic skills and stitches used remain the same throughout, making it a very versatile craft which is easily achievable with a few basic supplies.

It is a craft enjoyed by men and women of all ages and is one of the easiest embroidery crafts to learn. It can be used to easily decorate household items, to make unique and interesting clothing or to create special gifts and cards for loved ones. It is also an ideal craft to provide a relaxing, mindful break from the hustle and bustle of modern everyday life as it allows us to focus on the task at hand, loose ourselves in the little crosses and the methodical process of the needle going up and down through the cloth.

In this book I aim to cover many of the main aspects of cross stitch, from a beginner level upwards, so even those of you who have never done any form of needlecraft in the past can start to grow your skills without it seeming daunting or overwhelming. Soon you'll be sewing beautiful items for your home and friends, maybe even designing a few charts of your own and I hope you'll come to love cross stitch and it's benefits as much as I do.

PART 1

❀ A BRIEF HISTORY

Needlework has existed as long has there has been cloth to work on and thread to work with, and cross stitch has appeared as a stitch within embroidery design for a very long time, but it is only relatively recently that it has been used as the sole stitch in the design and become a craft in it's own right.

The earliest recorded evidence of cross stitch in needlework dates as far back as the 6th and 7th century after a fragment of cloth was discovered preserved in an Egyptian tomb.

During the Tang Dynasty, cross stitch was popular in China, often a females worth was elevated by her ability to sew clothes and embellish them with beautiful designs for her family so it became a desirable skill among women. It's likely that a desire for cross stitch spread West during this time along the silk trade routes and then later spread around the rest of the world in much the same way that anything else did, through migration, invasion and trading. Cross stitch as a craft form was easily adapted and incorporated into the traditions and cultures the individual countries around the globe.

The early designs were sewn without the aid of a pattern in the sense that we understand now. They were often passed down or recorded in the form of samplers. Originally samplers were not the decorative items we know today, and were not intended for display, they were stitches and designs worked on a piece of cloth that could be stored and were used to document the sewers favourite designs and stitches as a record to look back on for reference and ideas. Because linen was expensive, none of it was wasted, so every inch of the cloth would have had something sewn onto it. Often the individual stages of an intricate stitch were shown so that others could follow it and they could be used as a teaching tool, in much the same way as reference books with step by step photographs are used today, to teach young women the skills of sewing which was a very valuable skill to have before the industrial revolution.

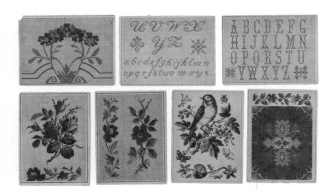

It wasn't until the 18th century that samplers changed into the decorative items that we recognise today. Items designed to be hung in the home often to show off a young stitchers achievements to visitors, while cross stitch was first practised in rural areas to embellish clothes and household linens, it was soon integrated into the culture of the upper classes. Having cross stitched ornaments on display in the home became a sign of wealth and young ladies were encouraged to add cross stitching to their list of accomplishments. It was around this time that cross stitch became the main stitch used within the designs and the patterns became more creative and elaborate, yet they often still remained a tool by which to teach lessons, but not only in sewing, they were also a way to teach young children their alphabet, numbers, to memorise religious verse and gain moral values.

The first recorded printed pattern book was produced in 1524 in Germany, but it was quite some time after this that pattern books became widely available. The early printed patterns were produced simply by printing black dots or squares on paper that the sewer could either count or prick through onto the fabric to produce the design, and the colours were always left up to the individual to decide upon, and it wasn't until 1890 when the first fabric made specifically for cross stitch was introduced.

During the 1st and 2nd World Wars cotton prices soared worldwide, when thread became a luxury item and not available easily to the public, combined with people having less free time, hobbies had to take a back seat and cross stitch went through a slump in popularity. Often at this time it was free hand embroidery that was favoured to document events and make tokens for loved ones and cross stitch lost favourability

It wasn't until the 1960's that cross stitch started to gain popularity again, when people found they had more leisure time. By this time cross stitch had changed much more into the modern craft form we recognise today, where it is increasingly popular to sew for pleasure, as a hobby and a way to relax, as well as to decorate our homes and produce gifts for loved ones.

WHAT IS CROSS STITCH?

Cross stitch in it's purest and most basic form is the art of creating pictures and words completely made up of "X" shaped stitches.

Passing the needle and thread diagonally one way and then the other to sew the two arms of the X and forming the cross shape. There is of course more to it than this, with lots of other stitch elements and details to learn, which I'll go into later, but this is essentially what cross stitch is.

Cross stitch is a counted thread form of embroidery, by which I mean the individual stitches are placed regimentally within the fabric as they are counted from a chart, it isn't sewn free style like many other styles of embroidery, so it requires a special fabric to sew onto which has been specifically woven to have a grid built into it, this keeps the individual cross stitches all the same size and the design can be sewn stitch by stitch and not become distorted. It is also usually sewn using a stranded thread that can be divided into different thicknesses to create different effects and textures.

Nowadays counted cross stitch is often sewn from a printed or digital chart which consists of a grid with coloured squares or symbols on it. Each of these squares or symbols informs the sewer which colour thread to use, what kind of stitch it is and where to place the stitch, allowing them to transfer the design from the chart to the fabric by means of counting and sewing.

All this no doubt sounds more complex than it actually is, but I'll expand on all these elements, the stitches, threads, fabric, other tools and the charts later in this book, as we progress through it and learn the craft step by step.

MATERIALS, TOOLS AND EQUIPMENT

You can start cross stitching with a few basic items, there is no need for lots of specialist equipment, although I'm sure you will acquire lots of things as you go along.

❀ ESSENTIAL EQUIPMENT

Needles

Fabric

Thread

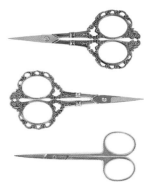

Scissors

❀ OPTIONAL EQUIPMENT WHICH YOU MAY FIND USEFUL

Hoop or Frame

Ruler or Tape Measure

Needle Threader

Fabric Pen or Pencil

Highlighters

Pin Cushion or Needle Minder

Thread Bobbins and Storage

In the following pages we'll look at these things individually and in a little bit more detail, so you can gain a better understanding and familiarity with them.

NEEDLES

Needles used to cross stitch are small tapestry needles. They are not sharp like standard sewing or embroidery needles, but instead have a blunt rounded end as they don't need to pierce the fabric, a standard sharp needle will often catch on the fabric, slowing you down and giving an uneven appearance to the crosses you are sewing. Also the blunt tapestry needles have a large eye, to accommodate various thicknesses of thread.

Cross Stitch needles come in a variety of sizes, the higher the number the finer the needle and the needle eye. The most usual sizes used in cross stitch are between 22 and 28 depending on the fabric count and how many strands of thread you are using. As a general guide as the thread count of the fabric goes up and becomes finer, so should your needle. We are essentially trying to match the needle to the fabric when we choose a needle to sew with, a large needle on a fine cloth would distort it and leave holes, similarly a fine needle on a low fabric count would be no good because it would become difficult to thread and handle. As a guide you can follow the chart shown opposite.

AIDA	EVENWEAVE	NEEDLE SIZE
6 count		18
8 count		20
11 count	22 count	22
14 count	28 count	24
16 count	32 count	26
18 count	36 count	28

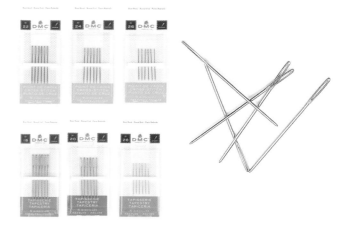

But it is very much down to trial and error and working out what works best for you and your needs. When you shop for needles you may come across different types and a few specialist ones that you may wish to invest in to try, so I'll mention a few here.

GOLD PLATED NEEDLES can be useful because they slip through the fabric easily, which can of course speed up your stitching a little, they are also very good because if you happen to leave your needle in your fabric for any time between stitching they should not mark the cloth.

TWIN POINTED NEEDLES, which are as the name suggests a needle with a point at both ends and the eye to thread located in the middle can be very useful as they allow you to sew without turning the needle round to pass it back through the fabric. They do take a little bit of getting used to, but again can speed up your sewing once you have practiced a little bit with them.

EASY GUIDE BALL-TIPPED NEEDLES are an ordinary cross stitch needle with a very small ball at the end, the ball helps you find the hole in the fabric easily and so stops the needle accidentality poking through the wrong part of the fabric or catching on your thread which helps make the stitches look smoother.

Although your cross stitch should be done with a blunt tapestry needle, you may also find it useful to have a sharp sewing needle too for when you are adding backstitch outlining, especially if you need to pierce a fabric block or cross stitch.

FABRIC

To ensure that the crosses in your sewing remain consistent cross stitch is sewn on a fabric that has an even grid structure built into it through having a consistent number of threads per inch in both the width and length (called the warp and weft), so that the design you are sewing doesn't become distorted and you can transfer the design from the chart to the fabric accurately.

This even gridded fabric comes in two main kinds, Aida and Evenweave. There are other things we can sew onto and you may encounter such as linen waste canvas, perforated paper, plastic canvas and even pre punched wood, which I'll cover briefly later, but for now it will be the two most common and widely used options that I'll talk about.

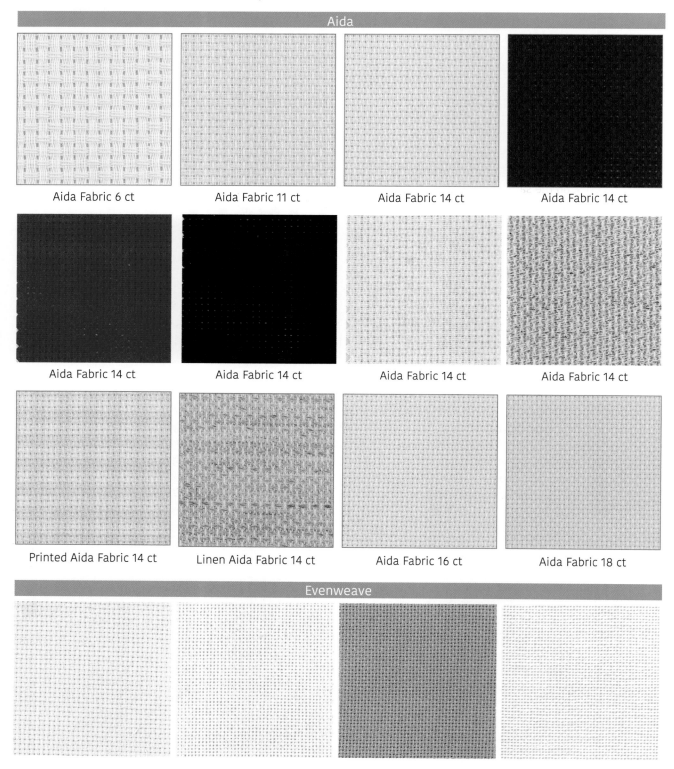

Aida

Aida Fabric 6 ct

Aida Fabric 11 ct

Aida Fabric 14 ct

Aida Fabric 14 ct

Aida Fabric 14 ct

Aida Fabric 14 ct

Aida Fabric 14 ct

Aida Fabric 14 ct

Printed Aida Fabric 14 ct

Linen Aida Fabric 14 ct

Aida Fabric 16 ct

Aida Fabric 18 ct

Evenweave

AIDA

Aida is probably the most common cross stitch fabric, and also the easiest to learn to cross stitch with. It is made up of four warp and weft threads woven together to form blocks with distinct holes which we sew through to form the cross. Every square on the fabric represents a square on the chart, so it is easy to see where your crosses should go. It comes in a variety of sizes, but 14, 16 or 18 count are probably the most common in cross stitch. The numbers refer to how many holes there are in an inch of that specific fabric, or I find it simpler to think of it as how crosses you can fit into an inch of fabric. As you can see from the diagram, the higher the aida count number the smaller the crosses become as you can fit more into one inch of cloth.

This consistency makes it easy to calculate how much fabric you need to complete the design you have chosen. Simply divide the total number of stitches in the width of the design by how many crosses you can fit into an inch (the holes per inch size) to find out the width of the fabric the design uses, do the same thing for the length and we know the total fabric needed.

For example, if your design is 36 stitches wide in total, and we are sewing on 14 count aida, then we divide the number of stitches by 14, because we can fit 14 stitches into every inch of cloth, to find the amount of aida the design takes up

$36 \div 14 = 2.57$

So if we are sewing on 14 count aida our design is 2.57 inches wide.

If we were using 18 count aida we would divide the number of stitches in the chart by 18, because we can fit 18 stitches in every inch now.

$36 \div 18 = 2$

So on 18 count aida the same design would be 2 inches wide.

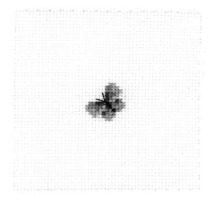

11 COUNT AIDA FABRIC
which is 11 stitches by
11 stitches in every inch

14 COUNT AIDA FABRIC
which is 14 stitches by
14 stitches in every inch

18 COUNT AIDA FABRIC
which is 18 stitches by
18 stitches in every inch

 # EVENWEAVE

EVENWEAVE is different to aida, and can be a little confusing to start with. It has the look to it much more like standard fabric, in that there isn't an obvious, visible grid to sew on, but it is there, woven into the fabric. Instead of it having a build in grid with blocks and holes like aida it has a set number of threads in it's warp and weft in every inch of fabric, so the count number refers to threads per inch rather than holes. To cross stitch on evenweave fabric we sew over 2 of these threads, so the count of the fabrics are higher. 28, 32 and 36 are the most commonly used. But as we are sewing over two threads of the fabric we can divide the thread count number by two. On 28 count fabric we can fit in 14 cross stitches across an inch of fabric, and so this becomes equivalent to 14 count aida.

This is particularly handy to remember when calculating size of fabric you need for any design and makes it less confusing and daunting.

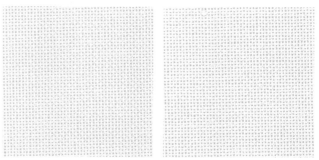

Evenweave 25 ct   Evenweave 28 ct

OTHER TYPES OF MATERIAL YOU CAN SEW ON

 WASTE CANVAS

is a useful material for sewing on regular fabric that doesn't have a grid structure such as clothing. You sew on it by simply placing it over the fabric you wish the design to be on, then sew through both layers using the grid on the waste canvas to place your cross stitches. Once you have sewn your design you can pull out the waste canvas threads leaving your sewn design behind on the fabric below, Soluble canvas is a similar product to waste canvas, except this dissolves in warm water leaving the design behind sewn onto your chosen fabric.

Waste Canvas

Waste Canvas

 PLASTIC CANVAS AND PERFORATED PAPER

are very similar, one being a stiff plastic with even holes punched into it, the other being a card with pre punched holes. Both can be useful for making 3D items which need to be stiff for their construction, or for making irregular items that you may want to cut out without the edge of the fabric fraying.

Plastic Canvas

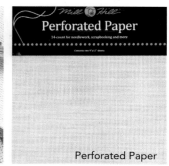
Perforated Paper

 PRE PUNCHED WOODEN SHAPES

are usually special shaped pieces of flat wood that have had holes punched into them which you sew through, they are most commonly used to make small items such as key chains or necklaces.

Pre Punched Wooden Shapes

SCISSORS

SCISSORS come in lots of different sizes and types, and you will probably find it useful to have a few different pairs available to you. But the most important ones you are going to need for cross stitching is a small, fine pointed pair of embroidery scissors for cutting threads close to the fabric when you are finishing off your stitching. The fine points will also come in very handy when the inevitable happens and you need to get underneath the stitches to cut and remove them after you have made a mistake or miscounted.

Other scissors which you will no doubt find useful to have handy are a larger pair, such as dress making scissors which are good for cutting your fabric to size and a general craft pair for cutting everything else, such as maybe trimming down a paper chart or cutting out templates.

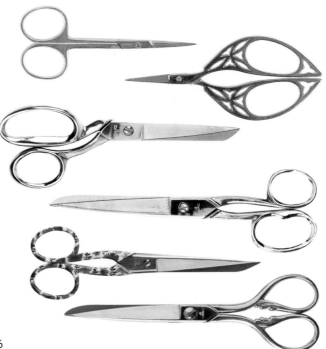

THREAD

The most common thread used for cross stitching is stranded thread, which comes in an abundance of colours and varieties, from solid dyed threads, to variegated and rainbow dyes through to more specialist threads such as glow in the dark, neon and metallics.

Nowadays there are many different thread companies producing threads, but you should always check if the threads are colour fast. Ones that aren't have no guarantee that they will not run should you need to wash your finished stitching, so this should always be taken into account when you are choosing a brand. If the thread you have does not state this on the label you can check it easily by pressing a clean damp white tissue to the thread for a few minutes, if you can see any trace of colour on the tissue when you remove it then the thread is not colour fast and extra care will need to be taken with it.

Stranded thread is so called because the thread is made up of six individual strands.

Most cross stitch is sewn using 2 of these strands, although this is just a guide, the chart you are using will give specific instructions for the amount of strands to use for each colour needed.

To sew with the thread we first have to divide it. Take a length of your chosen thread, about 40cm will be adequate, and holding the thread between your thumb and finger, spread the end out so the individual strands are visible. Taking hold of one strand with your other hand gently pull it out, the rest of the threads will gather up, but don't worry about this, they are easily straightened out afterwards.

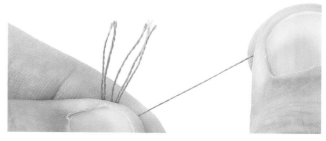

Do this again for however many strands you require for your stitching and then smooth them back together to sew with. Don't be tempted to try to pull out more than one strand at a time, this will more often than not result in the threads tangling and a lot of wasted thread.

✾ BLENDING FILAMENTS

You may also occasionally come across blending filaments, these are very fine metallic threads that in cross stitch are often combined with regular stranded thread to add a subtle shimmer, if a metallic thread would look too harsh. The individual chart will advise you how to combine them, but usually they are mixed one strand of a blending filament to either one or two strands of stranded cotton and these are then threaded through your needle together to sew with.

HOOP OR FRAME

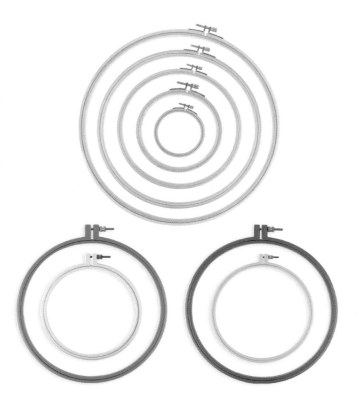

These are by no means essential but instead very much down to your personal preference. Many stitches only ever sew holding the fabric in their hand and others prefer to have the fabric held taught in a hoop or frame.

Often too there is no right or wrong time to use either a frame or a hoop. Frames can be very useful for larger projects, especially ones on stands as they support the weight of the fabric and they hold all the unused fabric neatly out of the way until you need it. They also allow the sewer to stitch using two hands, which is quicker once you become practised at it. But again this is very much down to personal preference. I myself swap between sewing in hand, in a hoop or using a frame depending on the individual project, so it is just a matter of trying different approaches to see which you prefer, but a 6 or 7 inch wooden hoop is a good place to start, it will hold your fabric taut, but not be too large to hold in your hand comfortably while you sew.

RULER OR TAPE MEASURE

This is of course invaluable for measuring fabrics before you cut them. A normal school ruler will suffice for most things, but a tape measure may also be useful for measuring larger areas, curves or more complex things.

NEEDLE THREADER

Needle threaders come in a variety of shapes and sizes but they are all especially useful when it comes to threading a very fine beading needle, or when you are threading any needle with satin or metallic thread with their springy texture. It can take a great deal of frustration out of the whole process of getting the thread through the eye of the needle.

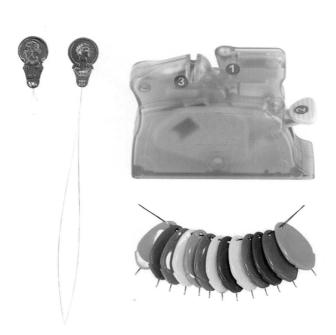

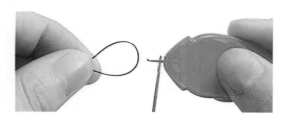

FABRIC PEN OR PENCIL

These are usually water soluble, or sometimes they can be removed from the heat of your iron. Your particular one will have manufacturers instructions so you know which one you have and how to remove it.

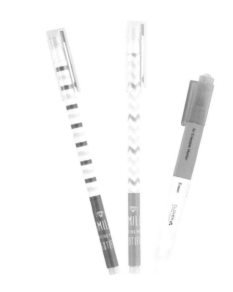

They are very useful to draw cutting lines or shapes onto your fabric to plan how it should be cut, it can save a lot of wasted fabric or the need to buy extra fabric to finish a project. They can also be used to mark a grid onto your chosen fabric if you prefer to sew onto a visible grid.

HIGHLIGHTER PENS

Basic office highlighter pens are a very useful tool and you should always have a few close to hand.

You can use them to highlight instructions on a chart which you need to pay particular attention to or of course you can colour the stitches you have sewn on the chart as you go so you don't lose your place and you can see how much you have sewn and how much is still left to do.

PINCUSHION OR NEEDLE MINDER

Pincushions are just that, tiny cushions that you can stick pins or needles into to keep them safe and so you know where they are when not in use. They come in lots of decorative finished and sizes so you're sure to find one you like that's right for you.

Needle minders come in all sorts of decorative designs too, but they are basically two strong magnets which you place on either side of your fabric as you are working. Out of the way in a corner the needle minder gives you a handy, safe place to store your needle while you are sewing, but unlike with pincushions your needle can still be threaded and attached to your fabric when stored, so they are particularly useful to store your needle safely if you need to put your stitching down before you have finished the length of thread in your needle.

THREAD ORGANISATION AND STORAGE

There are many different ways you will come across to organise the threads that you own and are using for a project.

You may decide that simply leaving them in the skeins they are sold in and organising them in a drawer, cabinet, box or project bag is what suits you best. But for those who don't want to do that, or want to try different methods there are lots of different methods out there and what works best for others might not work best for you. Often the level of organisation you need depends on how many different threads you own, how much space you have and also if you need to be able to find colours quickly by their type, brand or number.

To organise the threads for an individual project, sometimes thread holders or strand cards are the easiest way to keep all

the threads you need together, they are often what you will find provided in a cross stitch kit if you buy one.

Winding skeins of thread onto thread bobbins is probably the most popular way to store threads

Thread bobbins are flat, specially shaped pieces of plastic or card that you can wrap thread around to keep it tidy. You can buy little stick on numbers from some of the popular thread brands so you can identify the shade, or you could just write on the bobbin with a permanent pen. These can then be stored in a specifically designed storage box which has little compartments just the right size for the bobbins to sit in.

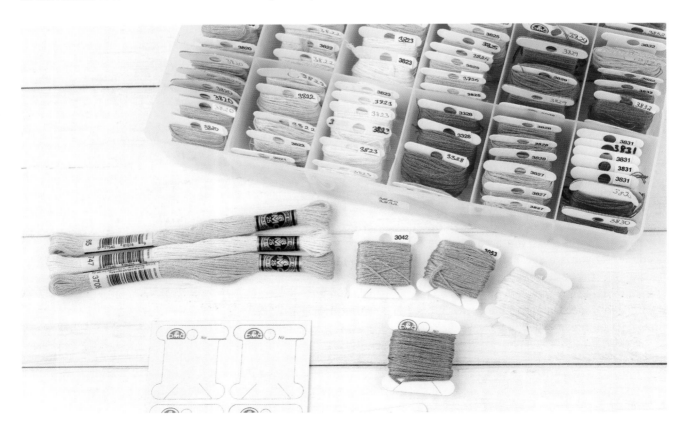

There are of course many other ways to store your floss, you may prefer to put the skeins onto stitch bows. These simply hold the whole skein in the shape it was bought in, so there is no winding to do, and you can then store them in a ring binder which comes with specially designed sleeves just the right size to hold the bows, so you can easily find the colour you need.

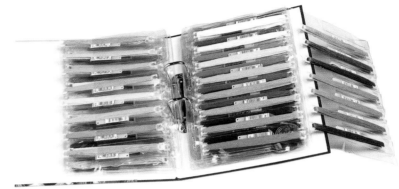

Floss Away bags are another good way to store your threads, they are small plastic bags with zip closures that have an area on them for you to write the details of the thread inside. They can then be sorted out into specific colours needed for a project and grouped onto a storage ring which is often provided with the bags. With these bags it's also very easy to store the spare strands you may have left over from a cut thread back into it's specific bag so it doesn't get wasted.

Whatever way you decide to organise your threads it is definitely advisable to do in one way or another once you have more than a handful of colours of thread types. So you can find the colours you need easily when you start a new project, and of course it avoids the inevitable tangles and wasted threads.

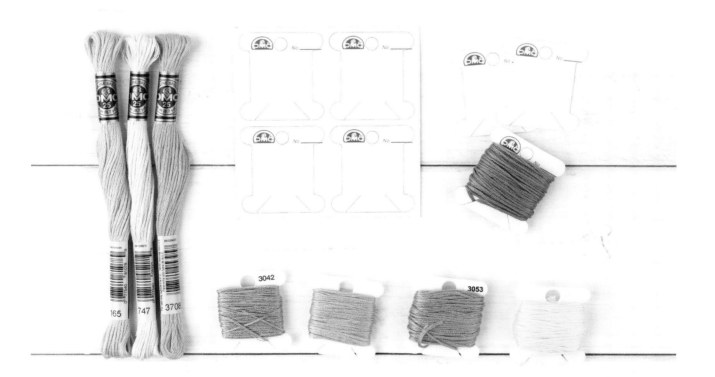

READING THE CHART

Before you can start sewing you will need to understand how to read a cross stitch chart and key. They are the instructions for how to transfer your design from the chart to the fabric.

Unlike most other types of embroidery, for cross stitch there is no design printed onto the fabric and we instead count the squares to transfer the stitches from the chart.

The cross stitch chart and key will tell you everything you need to know about what colour to use and where to stitch to complete the design. They can look confusing and overwhelming the more complex the design becomes, which is why it is important to start with something small and simple, that way you can get a feel for the process and you won't give up before you really start.

The chart grid is often numbered, with numbers running along the top and side this is just to ease counting and so you can see easily the size of the whole grid. The lines are also broken down with a bold line every 10 squares to form 10 x 10 sections, this is to make reading the chart and keeping your place easier, it looks less daunting than a solid grid with no breaks in it. The grid on the chart corresponds to the grid created by the weave of the fabric, each square on the chart whether it is filled or not represents one block on the fabric and each filled square represents one stitch.

Sometimes you will see the chart has coloured or tinted blocks behind the symbols or sometimes there are just black and white symbols shown for you to follow, but both types of chart are read in the same way.

The the squares on the chart will have a matching square in the key which will tell you what colour to use for that stitch, and also how many strands of thread to use to sew it.

Cross stitches will be shown on the key by blocks of colour, back stitch is usually shown by coloured lines and French knots and beads are shown with coloured dots, but I'll cover this later and in more detail when I go over the stitch types.

The chart will also often give you other useful information, such as the finished size of the stitching, recommended fabric to use, recommended needle size, what type of stitches are involved in the design and sometimes a difficulty level, so you can judge if the design is suitable for your abilities before you start it.

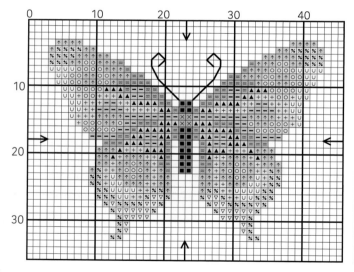

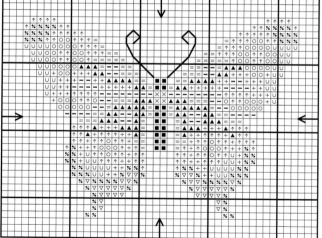

THE STITCHES

❀ WHOLE CROSS STITCH

The most basic stitch in cross stitching, and the place we'll start is of course with the cross stitch itself. Often you'll see these referred to on patterns or in kits as whole cross stitch.

Whole cross stitch is usually shown on the chart by a coloured square with a symbol, or just a symbol if it's a black and white chart. This will correspond to the same symbol in the chart key which will tell you what colour to sew the stitch and how many strands of thread to use.

The stitch is made up of two arms, a bottom arm and then a top arm, sewn on top of one another to form the cross shape. The main thing to remember when sewing these stitches is to keep all the bottom arms going the same way and all the top arms going the same way. It doesn't matter if your top arms all go / or \, so long as they are consistent. This will make sure your finished sewing has an even, smooth texture and just looks generally neater.

The whole cross stitch itself can be sewn in two different ways. Either as a whole stitch, where a complete stitch is worked before moving onto the next one, or as a row of bottom arms stitched in a line or group before completing the stitch with all the top arms on the return journey. Which method you choose to sew with is often just down to personal preference, however sometimes it's better to choose one method over the other. If you are sewing with variegated or hand dyed thread for instance then sewing one complete stitch at a time is the best way to keep the colour variations in the thread visible.

SEWING A COMPLETE CROSS STITCH

SEWING ON AIDA

Bring the needle up from the wrong side of the fabric at one corner of the block through the hole in the fabric and go straight across the block diagonally to the opposite corner to take the needle back down and sew the bottom arm of the cross stitch. Repeat this with the other two holes in the fabric block to sew the top arm and complete the cross stitch.

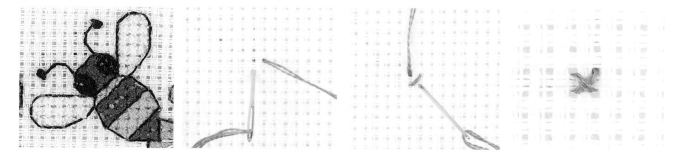

SEWING ON EVENWEAVE

The cross stitch is sewn in exactly the same manner on evenweave fabric as it is on aida, however because there is no distinct blocks to sew on we need to count the fabric threads. Bring your needle up in one of the spaces between the fabric threads, then count two fabric threads across and two down to go back down and create the bottom arm of the cross. Repeat this process in the opposite direction to complete the top arm of the cross stitch. This is often referred to as sewing over two, as you are taking your thread over two threads of the fabric weave.

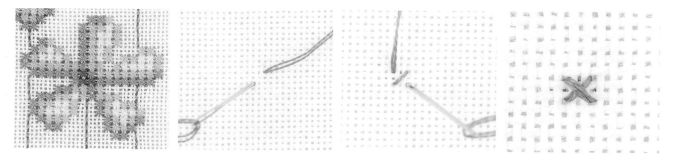

SEWING A WHOLE CROSS STITCH IN TWO JOURNEYS

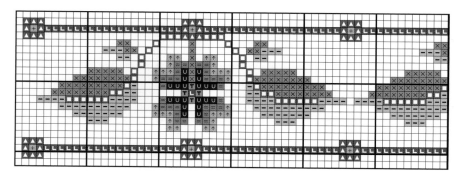

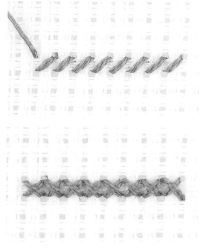

To sew a cross stitch in two journeys, you sew it in exactly the same way as you did the complete cross stitch, either going over one aida block or two fabric threads, however now we work a row of bottom arms only first, then complete the cross stitch on the return journey sewing all the top arms

❋ BACK STITCH

Back stitch is usually indicated on a chart by a solid black or coloured line which will correspond to the same line on the chart key, this will tell you what colour to sew that line and also how many strands of thread to use.

The back stitch should always be sewn last after you have completed all the cross stitch, to add definition and detail to the design.

Bring the needle up at 1 and go back down at 2, then up at 3 and back down again at 1 and so on, following the line drawn on the chart.

The back stitch can go in any direction, up, across or even diagonal and generally it's sewn over one aida block or two evenweave threads at a time.

Sometimes (which you will find as you progress onto more complex designs), the back stitch is longer, going diagonally across 2 or more squares, so the designer can create smooth curves and lines. This should be sewn as one long straight stitch, simply find the next logical point for the needle to go down, where the back stitch line and the grid line intersect. As a general rule it's fine to go across 3 blocks at a time, more than this and the thread can move and distort the design, so on a very long stitch you may need to half the stitch and pierce the middle of a block.

Alternatively on occasions where more detail is needed, the back stitches could be tiny, only going over half of a square, or starting and finishing mid square and not following the grid. This is perfectly fine, in this instance, simply follow the back stitch line as before, piercing the fabric where indicated on the chart. You'll find that switching to a sharp embroidery needle to do this sort of back stitch is very beneficial and saves a lot of struggling and frustration. It also increases the accuracy of you placed back stitch.

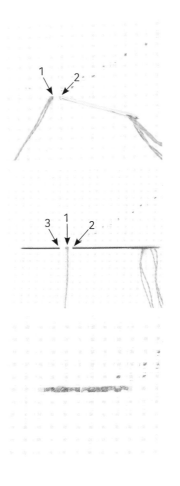

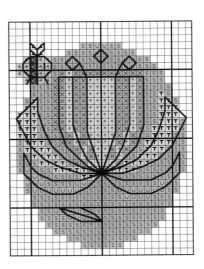

✿ HALF CROSS STITCH

Half cross stitch is sometimes confused with fractional stitches (which I'll talk about later), but it is a different stitch and is used for a different reason.

The half cross stitch is often used in the background of a design to fade out areas or give a painterly effect. Which is why you may often find the same colour of thread being used in whole cross stitch, then in half cross stitch using two strands of thread, then the same colour of thread being used again but this time the half cross stitches would be sewn using 1 strand of thread to complete the fade. It is a very simple stitch to sew, as it is as the name suggest just half a whole cross stitch. To sew it we simply have to sew one arm, but then leave it like this and don't add the second arm to complete the whole cross stitch.

Sometimes the chart you are following will tell you which way the half cross stitch is to face, if the designer wanted to achieve a certain result. If the design does not specify a direction then it is up to the sewer to decide which way the stitch should face and what they would like to achieve. As a general rule if you sew the half cross stitch so it follows the same direction as the top arm of your cross stitch it will blend in more, sewing it in the opposite direction will give much more contrast visually and texturally, making the areas stand out more this is worth considering when you decide which way you want the half cross stitch to face.

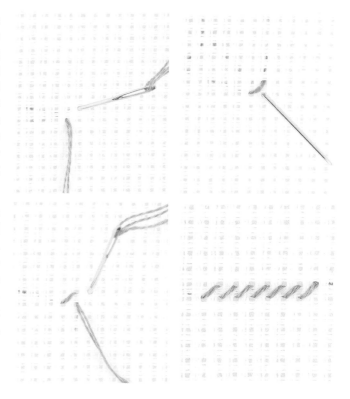

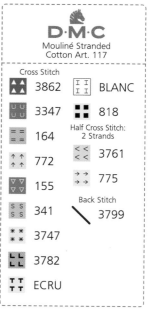

D·M·C
Mouliné Stranded
Cotton Art. 117

Cross Stitch

▲▲	3862	I I / I I	BLANC	
U U U	3347	▪▪ ▪▪	818	

Half Cross Stitch:
2 Strands

= = / = =	164	<< <<	3761	
↑↑ / ↑↑	772	→→ / →→	775	
▽▽ / ▽▽	155			

Back Stitch

S S / S S	341	╲ 3799
**	3747	
L L / L L	3782	
T T / T T	ECRU	

✿ FRACTIONAL STITCHES

There are quite a few different fractional stitches, and I'll go through them one my one, but they are all used for the same reason in a design, which is to allow the designer to add in more detail than a whole cross stitch would allow. They enable us to create smoother lines and curves and to produce a more delicate design.

The two kinds of fractional stitch that you will encounter most frequently are quarter stitches and three quarter stitches, both of these can be sewn together or individually and it can be a little confusing at first to decide which to use where, but given a little bit of experience and practice it will soon become second nature.

The diagonal fractional stitches are shown on a chart generally by a triangle that has the symbol for that stitch in one corner, sometimes the triangle isn't there, especially on some black and white charts, in which case just the symbol will be printed small in one corner of the chart square, but this should be read in the same way. All fractional stitch types are easier to sew on evenweave fabric than on aida, so if you see that the chart you are sewing has a large number of fractional stitches in it, I'd advise sewing that design onto evenweave. It is however possible to sew fractional stitch on aida, just a little harder to do.

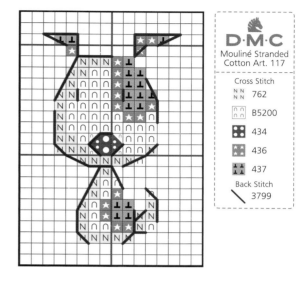

D·M·C
Mouliné Stranded Cotton Art. 117

Cross Stitch	
N N / N N	762
∩ ∩	B5200
⊞	434
★	436
⊥	437

Back Stitch	
╲	3799

QUARTER STITCH

The quarter stitch is as it suggests one quarter of a whole cross stitch. To sew this simply sew half of one of the cross stitch arms, depending on where you need to place it, bring your needle up at one corner of the block, but instead of taking your needle all the way across to the other corner, go down at the centre of the block to complete the quarter stitch.

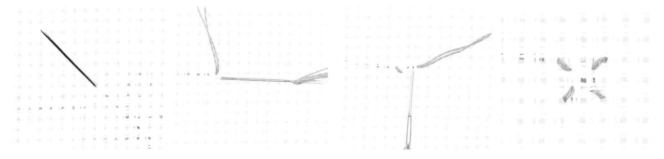

THREE QUARTER STITCH

The three quarter stitch is simply achieved by sewing three quarters of a whole cross stitch. First sew the short arm as you would with a quarter stitch, taking the needle down at the centre of the block, then sew all of the second arm of the cross stitch to complete the three quarter fractional stitch.

You may have noticed on the chart that quarter stitches and three quarter stitches look the same. This is often where the confusion arises, and when you are new to fractional stitches it can be hard to decide which to use where.

As a general rule if only one triangle is shown on the chart and the other half of the block is left empty, regardless of whether there is back stitch here or not, then that stitch should be sewn as a three quarter stitch. A single quarter stitch would appear empty and lost in the sewing, too much fabric would show through and the fractional stitches would become obvious instead of unnoticeable in the finished piece.

The only time a quarter stitch is generally used is when two fractional stitches occupy the same block. Then we need to decide which of the two colours is the dominant one. It is usually the stitch that is in the foreground, or the main colour. So for example if you have an object against a stitched background, the background would be the quarter stitch. Similarly if you have eyes or a mouth against flesh on a face, the eyes and the mouth are the main focus, so you would sew the face flesh colour as the quarter stitch.

Given a little time and experience deciding which stitch should be the quarter stitch and which should be the three quarter stitch will become second nature and you will be able to identify them easily on a chart.

SQUASHED FRACTIONAL STITCHES

As I mentioned earlier, quarter and three quarter stitches are the most common ones used in cross stitch. Although as your sewing progresses and you are learning more and tackling more and more complex designs you may also encounter squashed fractional stitches, which are sometimes also called squashed cross stitches. They are in fact just that, whole cross stitches that have been squashed to take up just a proportion of the block.

There are two types of squashed fractional stitches, vertical and horizontal. Which can sometimes be worked singularly or with two colours making up a block the same as with diagonal fractional stitches.

Both horizontal and vertical squashed fractional stitches are sewn in the same way as a whole cross stitch, but they only use up half of the block. Where the symbol is within the block determines where to place the stitch. Bring the needle up at one corner of the block, but instead of going diagonally across to the opposite side of the block, take the needle down at the half way point. Repeat this process to sew the other arm. The resulting cross stitch will be squashed and have a rectangular appearance instead of the normal square look of a regular whole cross stitch.

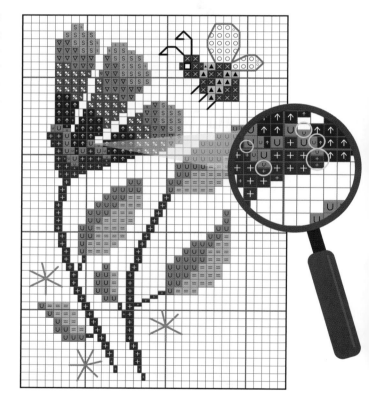

STRADDLED CROSS STITCH

A straddled cross stitch is simply a whole cross stitch sewn in the usual manner but it is placed to go across two or more blocks, rather than sit in it's own square on the gird it will straddle the gird lines.

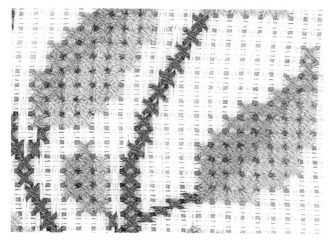

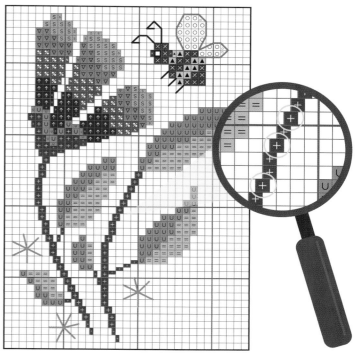

OTHER STITCHES AND TECHNIQUES

TWEEDING THREADS

Tweeding or blending threads is a very simple process of combining two or more threads in your needle at the same time. It's often used to create a two tone effect which can add texture and movement, or if the two threads are similar in colour and tone it can simply be used to create an extra colour that may not exist in the thread range so the designer can create a more natural blend between two shades.

It will be shown on the chart exactly the same as other whole or fractional stitch but it will have it's own symbol, and when you refer to the key for that particular colour you will see two or more numbers listed next to it and specific instructions for how many strands of each shade to combine together.

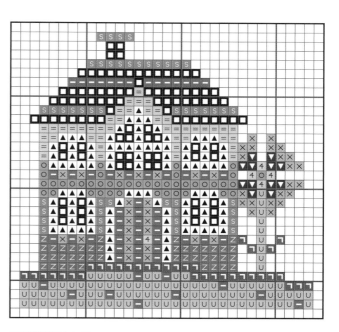

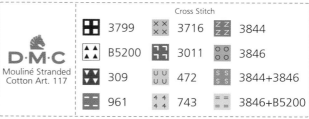

		Cross Stitch			
D·M·C Mouliné Stranded Cotton Art. 117	3799	3716	3844		
	B5200	3011	3846		
	309	472	3844+3846		
	961	743	3846+B5200		

29

❀ PETIT POINT

Sometimes in a design where the designer wants to add a lot of detail into a small space or make the sewing look finer, on a face for example. Then you will see up to four symbols taking up on square.

Usually this area will be given special instructions on the chart, either in the key or as a special note so you are aware or any particulars of how it should be sewn. They are most often to be sewn a tiny cross stitches, sewing only across one fabric thread instead of the usual two, but sewn in exactly the same way as a regular whole cross stitch.

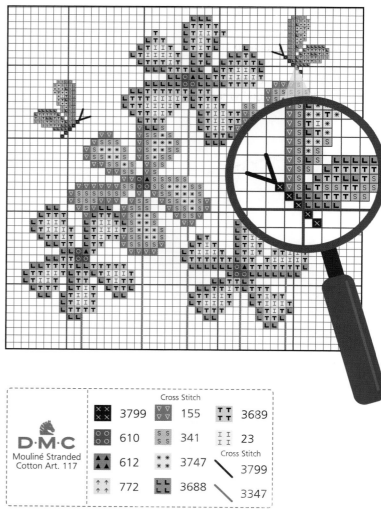

	Cross Stitch		
×× 3799	▽▽ 155	TT 3689
∘∘ 610	SS 341	II 23
▲▲ 612	** 3747	Cross Stitch
↑↑ 772	LL 3688	⟋ 3799
		⟋ 3347

D·M·C
Mouliné Stranded
Cotton Art. 117

❀ FRENCH KNOT

French knots are small stitches often used in cross stitch designs to add details or texture to objects such as flower centres. They are usually shown on a chart as a coloured dot that relates to the same coloured dot in the key where you will find specific information about the colour and the amount of strands to use to sew the stitch.

They can be tricky and frustrating when you first try them, and often sewers become scared of them before they even try to sew them, but once you've sewn a few you should have no trouble with them at all.

To sew a French knot, bring your needle up to the front of the fabric at the place indicated by the dot on the chart and holding the needle near the fabric, wind the thread around your needle twice. Pull the thread firmly but not too tight so the wraps sit snuggly around your needle. Re-insert your needle one fabric thread away from where your needle originally came up and keeping the tension on the wrapped thread gently pull your needle through to the back of the fabric. Your wraps should stay close to the fabric and keep nice and tight, to create a perfect French knot in the correct position.

It's important when doing French knots to not take your needle down through the same hole that you brought your needle up, but instead go one fabric thread or half an aida block over to prevent the French knot from potentially disappearing through to the back of your sewing and to hold the thread with your none sewing hand until it is nearly all through to the back to prevent the wraps around your needle from working loose.

If you wish to make the French knots bigger, then you should increase the number of strands used to make the knot, not the number of wraps around the needle which can often result in a messy loose knot.

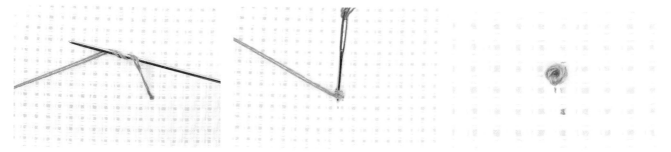

BEADS

Beads are often used in cross stitch to add a little bit of glitter and shine. Even a few added in the right place can make a finished stitching look much more opulent.

Beads can be represented on a chart in various ways depending largely on the type of bead and the chart manufacturers preference, so it is best to check your chart key to be sure. But often they are shown as a coloured dot with a smaller black dot inside, much like a bead would look with the hole going through it.

The most common beads used in cross stitch design are seed beads, which come in a large range of colours and finishes such as antique or frosted. They are usually around 2.5 mm in diameter, this is sometimes referred to as a size 11.0 bead on a chart, but most often they will simply be called seed beads. Seed beads are specially made for needle work and have a uniform shape and size so they look consistent on your sewing.

When you see the seed beads you will notice they are very small, with a very small hole running through them. This is why we need a very fine beading needle, or very small needle to attach them. The beads are normally attached using two strands of thread in a similar shade to either the bead, or the fabric which can be more convenient if

you have lots of random coloured beads to attach. You can also buy specific beading thread, which with it's slightly invisible appearance is suitable for sewing on any bead.

You will find that some charts have stitches under the beads, so the beads stand proud of the design. Other times the beads are sewn directly onto the fabric, which will be indicated on your chart. But however they are placed they should be sewn on last after the cross stitch and the back stitch so they don't get in the way.

There are various ways to attach a seed bead, the most usual way is to simply use a cross stitch to add the bead to the design. Bring the needle up in the usual manner to sew the first arm of the whole cross stitch, but before going back down to finish the arm add on the bead. Then use the second arm of the cross stitch to secure the bead, bringing the needle up at the usual place, but before taking it back down to complete the arm, split the two strands so one strand of threads falls on each side of the seed bead. This will help to hold the bead in place and stop it moving about.

❋ OTHER TREASURES

As well as being able to add beads to stitching, there is of course a whole wealth of other things you could add. Often you can buy charts that come with specific chart packs that contain all sorts of pretty charms and beads. In these instances specific instructions would be given for how to attach them depending on the designers preferences.

But if you wish to experiment with adding things to your stitching then anything not too large can be sewn onto fabric. Sequins, metal or wooden charms and buttons are a good place to start as these usually have holes or a loop for them to be easily attached to the fabric. Sequins in particularly can look very beautiful and can be attached in in a number of ways. You could sew a French knot through the central hole, thread a bead onto your needle before going back down through the central hole in the sequin, you could sew the sequin on with eyelets or with a series of back stitches, so that depending on how you sew them on the look of the sequin can be changed to suit your design making them very versatile.

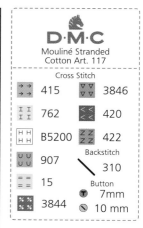
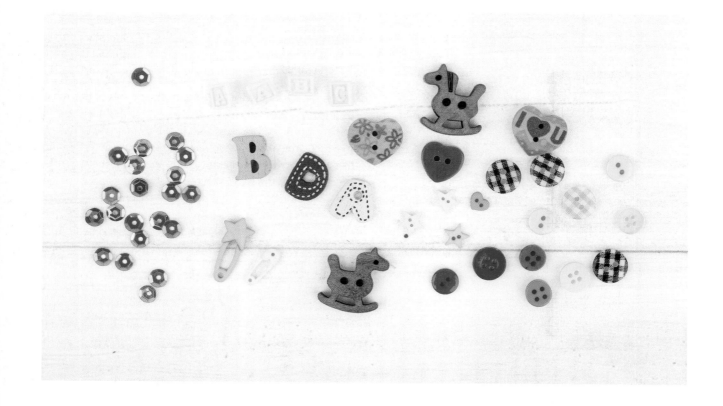

✽ EYELETS

As you expand your cross stitch knowledge or encounter more designs and charts you may see that designers sometimes utilise stitches which aren't cross stitch design stitches, but rather embroidery stitches that can be sewn as a counted thread embroidery stitch.

Probably the most common one you will encounter is the eyelet, which is often used to depict stars, snowflakes or just to add texture and pattern. Eyelets can come in a variety of shapes and sizes, so you would need to follow your chart for the placement and size, but they are always sewn in the same way.

You should always sew the arms of the eyelet in one direction, bringing the needle up at the outer most edge of the eyelet before taking it down at the centre, to then bring the needle up again at the next adjacent arm. Always taking the needle back down through the same central hole and working round the arms in order.

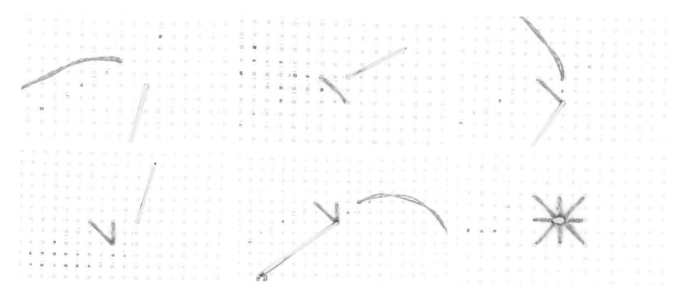

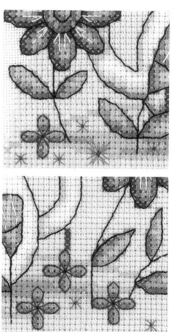

✳ ✳ 3607 - eyelets
sewn using 1 strand

✿ DOUBLE CROSS STITCH

The double cross stitch is a variation of a standard cross stitch and they are often used to add texture or a slightly raised effect on a border for example.

To sew the double cross stitch first you need to sew a standard whole cross stitch, but before moving onto the next stitch bring your needle up at the halfway point of the block between the two bottom arms and take it straight up and back down between the arms at the top of the block fo sew a vertical line. Repeat this to sew a horizontal line so you have an upright cross stitch "+" sewn over the top or a regular "x" cross stitch to form the double cross stitch.

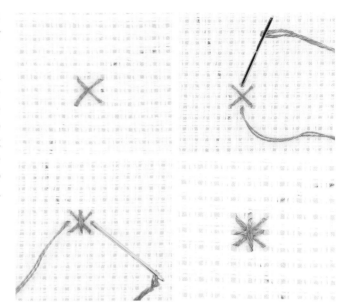

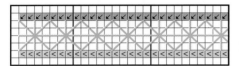

4502 - Coloris thread double cross using 2 strands

✿ LAZY DAISY

The lazy daisy is another stitch that you may encounter in cross stitch designs, especially if you sew designs that contain small flowers, as as the name suggests it is a very quick and easy way to embroider flowers as well as add texture and interest to a cross stitch design.

It is merely a number of individual chain stitches arranged into a circular flower shape. It can be shown on the chart in a number of ways, but often it will simply be a series of lines radiating out from a central point to indicate where to bring your needle up and take it back down.

First bring your needle up at the inside point of one of the lines and take it back down right next to where you brought it out, but without pulling your needle all the way through bring it back out at the point indicated at the other end of the line on your chart. Now with your needle still in the fabric, loop the thread around the needle and then pull your needle through to the front of the fabric, before taking it back down just above the top of the loop you have sewn to anchor it in place.

This forms the first isolated chain stitch. Continue in this way where indicated by the other lines in the circle on the chart to complete the lazy daisy stitch.

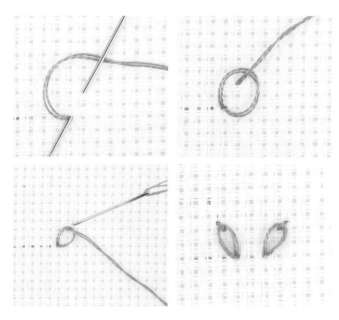

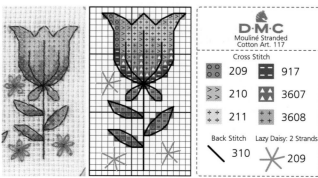

MAKING A START

Now we have covered threads, fabric, materials and looked at stitch types we are ready to make a start with the sewing.

First we need to choose the project you wish to sew. If you are an absolute beginner I'd suggest choosing a small design which contains only whole cross stitches from this book, and using the key that is always near to the chart sort out which particular threads you need and also the other materials which will be given in a materials list.

To begin we need to find the centre of the design, sometimes this is marked on the chart, but if not simply count halfway along the length and width of the chart and add a small mark. You can find the centre of your fabric by folding it in half and half again and making a small crease in the centre. Now when we start stitching we will

know the centre of the chart will be in the centre of the fabric and we will not run out of room one way or another on the fabric for the design. There's nothing worse than getting quite a way through a design, only to realise you have misplaced the design on the fabric and that you will run out of fabric before you have completed the design.

Now we've found the centre of the fabric and the design and we have separated out the correct number of strands for your first stitch it's time to start.

There are various ways to start your sewing, but two of the most popular ones are either starting with a loop stitch or waste knot, so I'll cover both of these.

❀ LOOP START

To start sewing in this way you need to take a single piece of thread, if your sewing requires two strands, and fold it in half to form a loop, then thread your needle with the two loose ends.

Bring your needle up where your first stitch is on the fabric and take it across and down in th appropriate hole to complete the first arm of the cross stitch, but before pulling the thread all the way through, turn your sewing over and pull the needle through the loop in the thread to catch and secure it. You can then continue on with our stitching in the normal way.

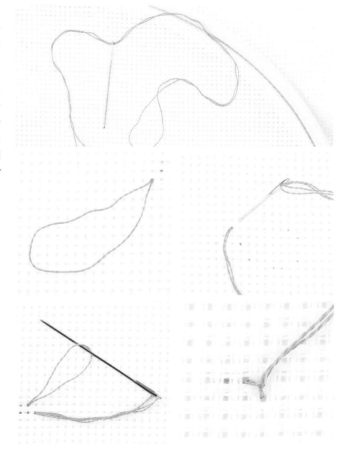

❁ WASTE KNOT

To start sewing using a waste knot, you'll need two strands of thread (or however many your design requires) and you simply tie a knot in the end of the thread. Then go down through the fabric from the front to the back a little way from where your stitching will start. If it's a line of crosses going horizontally from left to right, then place the waste know just a little bit further to the right than your stitches.

Now when you bring your needle to the right side of the fabric to start your first stitch the thread has created a very long straight stitch on the back of the fabric. As you start sewing you should catch this long stitch with your cross stitches to hold it in place.

Once you've make a few stitches you can gently cut the knot off, pull the loose thread to the back and neatly trim any extra away. You can now continue with the rest of your sewing in the usual way.

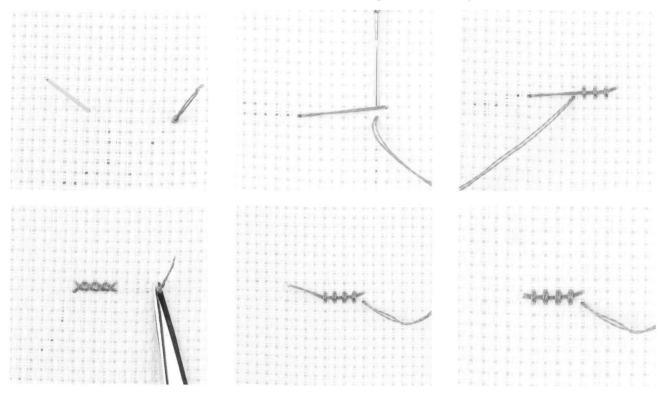

FINISHING A LENGTH OF THREAD

At some point in your sewing, you'll either come to the end of your length of thread, or want to change to a different colour and need to change thread. To do this you need to first finish off the thread you are using.

This is a very simple process, just turn your work over to the back and take your needle under 3 or 4 stitches before pulling the thread through, trimming any extra off close to the fabric. Your thread is now finished securely and tidily without creating any lumps or bumps.

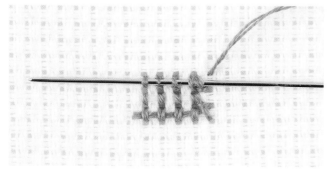

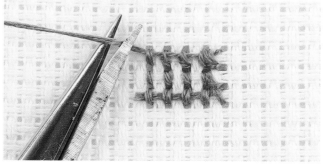

A NOTE ABOUT THE BACK

Often it is said that the back of your work should be as neat as the front. I'd say yes and no to this.

Yes because it is important to have a tidy back to your work, simply for practical reasons. If the back is tidy, without knots or lumps it will lie flat and be easier to deal with later when it comes to finishing or framing. It's also easier to sew on a piece that doesn't have lots of trailing or loose threads to catch you up and get you tangled, and of course lots of tangles and loose threads at the back is just a waste of thread. You'll find a project will take a lot more thread to complete it if you sew in a more untidy manner, which can be a problem if you are sewing from a kit with specific supplies.

But I also said no because ultimately I want cross stitch to be enjoyable, rather than a chore. So I'd say don't stress too much about the back, most of the time it won't be seen anyway, just do your best, and as you learn and progress the back will naturally become tidier.

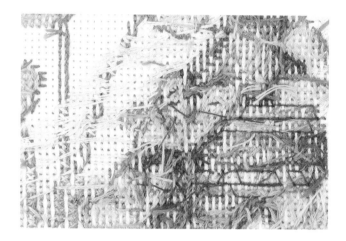

WASHING YOUR SEWING

Often once you have finished your cross stitch piece, especially if it is something you have been working on for a long time, you will want to wash it. Only ever wash your sewing though if you are sure the threads are colourfast, there's noting worse than spending a long time on a piece only to ruin it because the colours run when you wash it.

You should always wash each cross stitch piece separately, never wash a few together or with other items.

First rinse the stitching under cold running water to wet it, then fill a sink or bowl with a small amount of a mild detergents like SOAK® which is suitable for sensitive textiles and either cold or luke warm water. Wash the sewing gently, if it has stains that you are trying to remove you may need to soak it, but never scrub the sewing or treat it harshly. Then rinse it several times in cold water until all the detergent is removed and the water runs clear.

Never wring out your sewing, it will distort very easily whilst wet. Instead sandwich it between two clean towels and roll it up like a Swiss roll to press out some of the water. Unroll and then lay your sewing onto a fresh dry towel to air dry until it's just damp when it will be ready to be ironed.

To iron your sewing place it right side down on another clean towel and press lightly with a warm iron and a pressing cloth. You can also use FLATTER® , a smoothing spray before ironing for easy wrinkle release. The steam will not damage the stitching, and placing it face down on a towel will prevent any of your stitches or beads from becoming squashed and damaged.

It's worth remembering to take special care when you iron work that contains sequins or other treasures. Be sure to not set your iron too hot, especially with sequins as they are often made form plastic and could melt and ruin your sewing.

GENERAL STITCH TIPS

CHECK YOUR CHART

Check your sewing against your chart regularly to avoid letting mistakes go unnoticed and creating larger areas to unpick and put right

GRIDDING YOUR FABRIC

On a larger design you may find that gridding your fabric is useful (pre-gridded fabric can also be bought). Gridding essentially duplicates the bold chart grid lines onto the fabric to help with counting. To grid your fabric you can either task stitch lines every 10 blocks or draw them on with an embroidery pen that is designed to wash out.

PHOTOCOPY PAPER CHART

If you have a paper chart, you may find it useful to photocopy it so you can colour it in as you go, which helps you keep a track of your stitching and avoid mistakes. This can also be an easy way to enlarge your chart too.

GOOD LIGHT

When sewing onto black or darker fabrics be sure to do so in a good light, also placing a light coloured cloth on your knee or table behind the fabric you are sewing onto can help the holes in the fabric show up much easier.

RAIL ROADING

As you progress and gain experience you may want to give rail roading a try. This is a technique to separate the two strands of thread you are sewing with and to help them to lie flat and parallel to each other. To do this as you sew simply pass the needle between the two strands of thread as you go back down into the fabric.

PRESS YOUR FABRIC

Press your fabric before you start to remove any creases, This will not only help you see the holes in the fabric, but also help you to spot any blemishes on the fabric that you may have otherwise missed.

HAVE FUN WITH YOUR CRAFT

Most importantly, remember to have fun with your craft and don't get stressed too much about the right way to do something, just have enjoy it and relax.

MARK THE TOP OF THE FABRIC

It can be useful to mark the top of the fabric (well away form your sewing area) with a mark so you can always identify the top of the sewing. I generally put a "T" in the top left, so I know which way up to start again if I've put the design down for some time, which can be very useful when the design just looks like groups of random stitches with nothing specific identifiable.

SEWING WITH VARIEGATED

When sewing with variegated or hand dyed threads complete one cross stitch at a time to keep the colours and shades separate on the cross stitches and never use the loop start method to sew with these threads, always pull out two threads from the cut length of thread so the dye pattern is the same on each strand.

PROTECT THE FABRIC EDGE

If you are sewing a design that may take you some time or be a long term project you should protect the fabric edge from fraying. You can do this either by edging your fabric with a zig-zag stitch, by using and acid free masking tape folded over the edge or by applying a small amount of a glue made specifically for this purpose such as Fray-Stop.

BE ORGANISED

Be organised, not just with your threads but with individual projects too, if you have more than one project you are working on at once keep the supplies you need for each one separate in it's own project bag or folder, this will save you a lot of time and frustration moving between your sewing.

DON'T JUMP TOO FAR

When you are sewing, don't jump too far from one area to another on the back of your work. The loose threads and loops will cause problems and look unsightly. If you are going more than 2 or 3 stitch spaces either finishing and cut off the thread, or weave the thread underneath the stitches already there to the next area. If it's a very big jump I'd always finish and restart just to save the thread from being wasted.

HANDS ARE FREE

Always make sure your hands are free not only of dirt, but also grease and oils before you start sewing. Your hands may look clean, but an extra wash can't hurt.

THREAD TWIST

Your thread will naturally twist as you sew, so every now and again let your needle hang from your sewing so it twirls itself straight again, this will avoid unnecessary tangles and knots.

THREAD CONDITIONER

When working with satin or metallic thread you may find a thread conditioner to be very useful to help the threads travel through the fabric easier and to relax them slightly and stop them springing about so quite much.

DISTORTED FABRIC

If your fabric has become distorted while you were sewing, and you find it is no longer square when you have finished, it is possible to stretch it slightly back into shape while the fabric is damp and pliable. This process is referred to as blocking. To do this dampen the cross stitched piece and after the water has soaked in to relax the fabric threads carefully tug the corners and sides of the canvas to gradually reshape it. Then pin the four corners of the fabric to a blocking board and gently pull and pin all the way around the sides to hold the fabric square as it dries.

USING A HOOP

If you are sewing using a hoop, remove it after each sewing session to avoid undue creases and marks on the fabric.

To minimise marks and to help the hoop grip your fabric you may find it useful to bind your hoop. Do this by wrapping a white binding tape around either just the inner hoop or both the inner and outer hoops and securing it neatly with a few stitches.

PART 2

LOOKING AT COLOUR

The world around us is full of colour and the world of cross stitch and threads is no different. You will find an abundance and sometimes overwhelming amount of colours on offer, so it's important to have at least a basic understanding of colour and how they interact together to give various effects. This is particularly important of course when it comes to designing or adapting charts to your own personal preferences.

There are a lot of books and information available regarding colour theory, and I can't cover everything here, but we can look at the basics and provide you with enough information to feel a little more confident when choosing threads. Of course nothing beats actually putting your chosen threads together and deciding if you like what you see, but a little knowledge will cut down significantly on the time it takes you to make these initial thread choices. It will give you a sense of what will and won't work together and allow you to choose threads accordingly and efficiently.

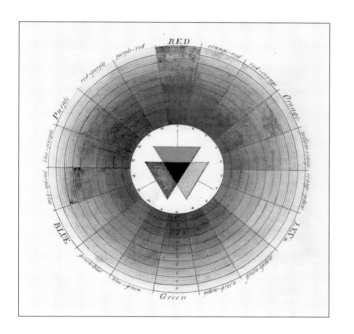

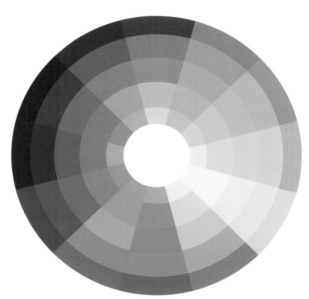

THE COLOUR WHEEL

The colour wheel based on red, yellow and blue is very traditional in the field of art and design, it was developed by Sir Isaac Newton in 1666 and is a good place to start when explaining colour.

PRIMARY COLOURS

The three primary colours are red, yellow and blue. These are the three pigment colours that cannot be mixed by any combination of the other colours. All other colours are mixed from these three primary pigments.

SECONDARY COLOURS

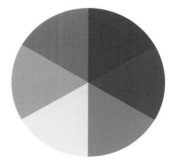

The three secondary colours are green, orange and purple and as you can see by the colour wheel these are formed by mixing together the primary colours that sit on either side of it.

TERTIARY COLOURS

The six tertiary colours are yellow-orange, red-orange, red-purple, blue-purple, blue-green and yellow-green and as shown in the colour wheel these are achieved by mixing together a primary and a secondary colour together to form a new colour.

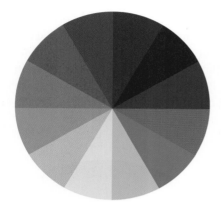

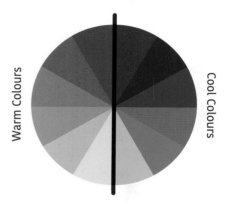

This set of 12 primary, secondary and tertiary colours forms the basic set of colours and can easily be divided into warm and cool colours. The warms are the reds, oranges and yellows and take up one side of the colour wheel. The cools are the purples, blues and greens and form the other side of the wheel.

Straight away we can start to see how we associate different colours with different feelings and emotions and how this would affect a design. Warm colours as the name suggests tends to make us think of warm and hot things such as the sun, fire and heat but they are also associated with brightness, positivity and energy. Cool colours by contrast evoke feelings of snow, ice, water and sky and are often associated with feelings of calm and peace.

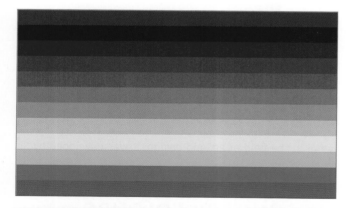

There are of course many, many more colours and shades of thread available for us to use than these twelve basic colours. So we now need to look at hue, shade, tint and tone.

Hues are simply the original pure colours.

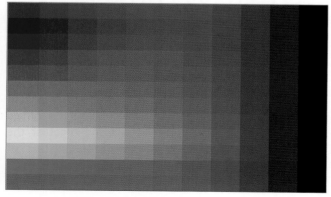

A shade is a hue to which we have added black, which has the effect of darkening the original colour.

A tint is a hue to which we have added white, which has the effect of lightening the original colour.

A tone is a hue to which both white and black (or grey) has been added, which has the effect of darkening the original hue but also makes it less intense.

With all these things taken into account you will see we can have an almost endless array of colours which are only limited by our ability to mix pigments or in the case of cross stitch, the colours that the manufacturers of thread can reliably mass produce, but you'll still find more than enough to choose from.

COLOUR SCHEMES

When choosing a palette of threads to work with it can be useful to understand from where on the colour wheel to choose the colours from, which to team them up with which other colours and how they would work together.

There are of course millions of possible colour combinations, and you can combine the colours any way you wish in your design, but there are some that work better than others and are more acceptable to a wider audience.

Often these will be instinctive to you already without you even knowing why, other than they look right. The right colour choices can focus the attention of the viewer where you want it to be whilst balancing the rest of the design. These are called colour schemes and designers often use them, sometimes subconsciously, sometimes planned to create the effect they want to in their designs.

To help you make your own colour choices I'll briefly go over some of the most common colour schemes which designers use.

MONOCHROMATIC COLOUR SCHEME

This is the most basic colour scheme. It uses only one dominant colour along with it's tints, tones and shades. Monochromatic colour schemes work well as a colour palette but it can be difficult to make them work in practice.

It can sometimes be difficult to tell parts of a design apart, to add contrast or give particular emphasis to one element. So the shades that you choose when working with a monochromatic palette need to be carefully considered.

ANALOGOUS COLOUR SCHEME

This colour scheme is made up of colours directly next to each other on the colour wheel and can create an attractive design that is pleasing to look at and easy on the eye. However there often isn't much contrast created between the hues, so this needs to created with other elements such as tints and shades.

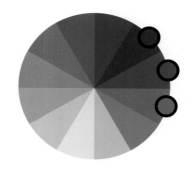

COMPLEMENTARY COLOUR SCHEME

Complementary colour schemes are made up of colours directly opposite each other on the colour wheel. When these colours are placed next to each other it produces a very vibrant contrasting effect which can look clashing and become hard to look at. When using this colour scheme tones need to be considered carefully and often it's best to use one colour as the dominant colour and use the other colour as an accent.

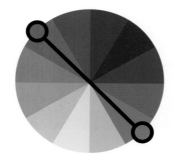

SPLIT-COMPLEMENTARY COLOUR SCHEME

A split-complementary colour scheme is a variant of the complimentary colour scheme but it uses one base colour and the two colour immediately next to it's compliment. This has the effect of still having a high degree of contrast between the two colours, without them looking as extreme as the complementary colours. They become less clashing and more harmonious to look at.

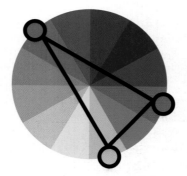

TRIADIC COLOUR SCHEME

Triadic colour schemes are made up of colours that are evenly placed around the colour wheel in the shape of a triangle. They tend to be dramatic colour palette with lots of contrast, whilst being one of the safer and more basic colour scheme options.

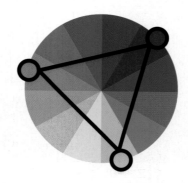

RECTANGULAR COLOUR SCHEME

Rectangular colour schemes are made up of four colours positioned around the colour wheel in the shape of a rectangle and can be one of the harder colour schemes to get right. However when it is done right it can be very rewarding and offers the contrast of opposites whist also making the design appear balanced and pleasing to look at.

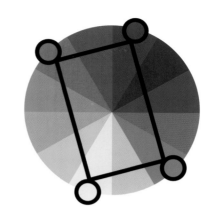

Nowadays however, with the vast array of information on the internet if you are not feeling confident choosing colours for yourself, or want some extra help or inspiration, there are many websites and apps to either help you or from which you can choose pre-determined colour palettes.

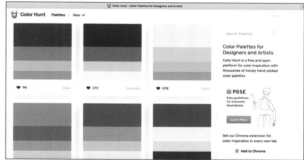

While these aren't giving you thread colours they are a good start for you to choose your threads from. If you are starting to adapt bought charts or design your own charts from scratch I'd recommend that you buy at least one manufacturer's thread shade card, which contains actual thread samples rather than printed representations of the thread so you can see the full selection of threads on offer to match your palette colours to.

ADAPTING AN EXISTING CHART

Sometimes you might see a kit or cross stitch chart that is almost right, but not quite. You might want to replace a small motif, change the colours or add personalisation with a name or dates for example. In this section I'll look at making basic but effective changes to an existing pattern so you can make it personal to yourself.

MAKING COLOUR CHANGES

Colours are the easiest way to make a design personal to you. You could change a birth sampler from blues to pinks for example or change the hair and skin tone of a girl on a design to match a family member. To do this first you need to look at the pattern you wish to alter and it's key to see how many colours you wish to change.

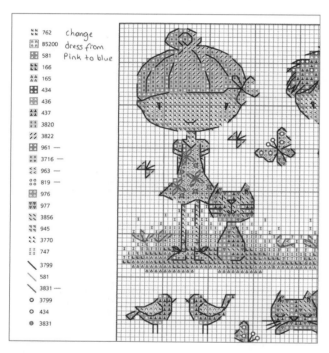

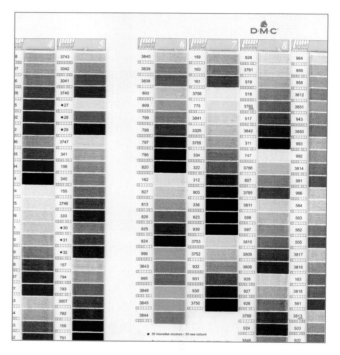

For this example we will use the girl chart available in this book and change the pinks to blues. First you need to identify all the colours that need to be changed, then for every colour you wish to change in the original pattern, you will need to find a similar one tonally in the new colour. For example, you would replace a light green with a light blue or a dark green with a dark blue, so you keep the visual tonal balance of the original chart.

Thread shade cards usually group the shades and tones of colours together, so if you can use a shade card, or even just view one on the company's website, this would make it much easier for you to easily make your colour selections.

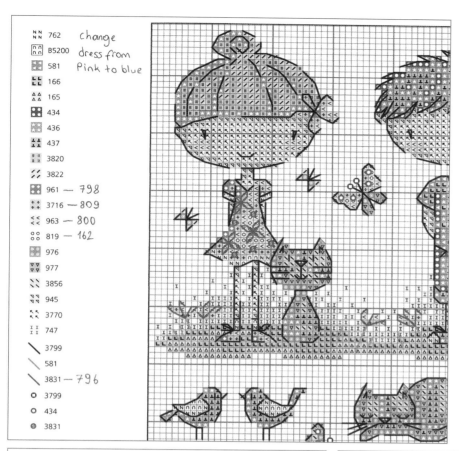

N N / N N	762	*change dress from Pink to blue*
B5200		
581		
L L / L L	166	
▲▲ / ▲▲	165	
434		
436		
437		
3820		
⁄⁄ / ⁄⁄	3822	
961	— 798	
3716	— 809	
≶≶ / ≶≶	963 — 800	
°° / °°	819 — 162	
976		
▽▽ / ▽▽	977	
╲╲ / ╲╲	3856	
⟍⟍ / ⟍⟍	945	
⟨⟨ / ⟨⟨	3770	
I I / I I	747	
╲	3799	
╲	581	
╲	3831 — 796	
O	3799	
O	434	
◉	3831	

Now once you have chosen your colours you can simply write these new colour selections along side the original key listings, then use these new thread colours when you sew the chart, there is no need to change the original chart in any way, you simply substitute the new colour for that symbols while you sew.

On the example I changed all the pinks into blue, but you could also just change sections such as her dress, or a butterfly and leave the rest in the original colour, it's up to you to do whatever you want.

CHANGING A MOTIF

Another way to personalise a chart is to change a small motif within it. Maybe the design you have features a small image of a cat and you would prefer a dog. This is a little trickier, but certainly still achievable. I would however recommend that unless you are quite confident with changing designs it's best to stick to swapping motifs on samplers or designs where the background directly around the motif you wish to change is very simple. Trying to swap a motif that sits on top of another complex design can just create too many problems and can take a long time to do as you have to readjust everything around the changed motif.

If the motif you want to swap is not interacting with anything else on the design, you can simply swap one for the other as you sew, you simply need to find a motif more of your liking in a similar size. Motif library charts and books can be very useful for substituting elements as they offer a selection of small individual motifs, usually grouped into themes to add to other existing charts.

But if on the other hand the motif to remove is placed on a background or is interacting with other elements in anyway, you may find it useful to trace new motif onto a sheet of graph paper, so you can fill in and make any changes that occur to the chart immediately around it. This will allow you to plan and position it just how you want it before you sew it.

18 sts

10 sts

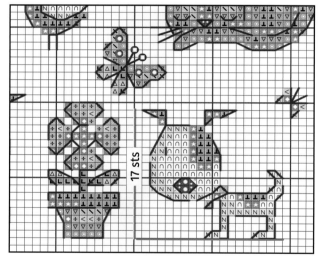

17 sts

For the example here I'll again use the girl and cat design featured in this book, and we'll swap her cat for a dog. First you need to measure the area on the chart that the motif you wish to take out uses. This will determine the size of the design you need to replace it with.

Next draw an area slightly outside the area the cat takes up on the chart and trace this onto a new sheet of graph paper, so you can see the area without the cat in it.

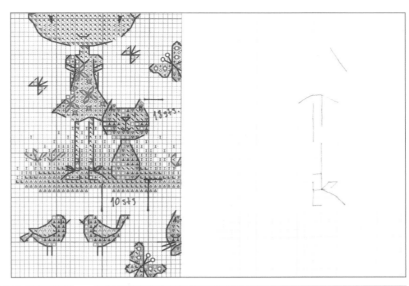

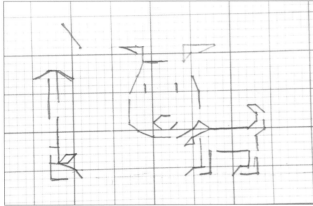

Now you need to draw the dog in where you want him to stand. I've placed him away from the girl rather than overlapping, but this will mean there is some of the girls

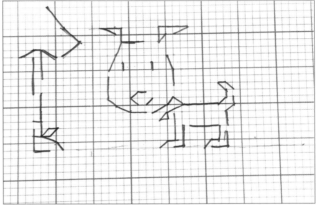

dress missing, so now looking at the other side of the dress for guidance you can draw in the missing area.

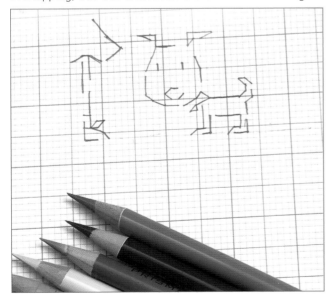

Now to fill in the missing cross stitches choose coloured pencils or pens in similar colours and simply colour in how you would like the chart to look.

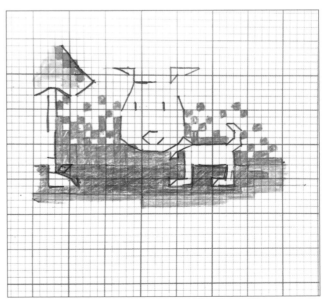

Your chart is now ready to sew using the original two and the new drawn one.

PERSONALISING WITH A NAME OR DATE

You can also personalise an existing chart by adding on names or dates. You could do this with any chart, simply by adding it in at the top or the bottom after first calculating the new size of the chart and adjusting the size of the fabric you are sewing the design onto. But often especially with birth or wedding samplers the designer will provide an alphabet and numbers with the chart and there will be a specific space on the chart to place the details.

To personalise a name or date on a chart you'll need to have the original chart, some graph paper, pens and a rubber handy.

Then using the alphabet chart supplied with your design, copy out the letters you need placing them along a line and allowing a little space between each one.

Usually one square between letters is enough of a gap, but this will differ depending on the style of the letters. You can look at the stitched example that should be with your chart as a guide to do this.

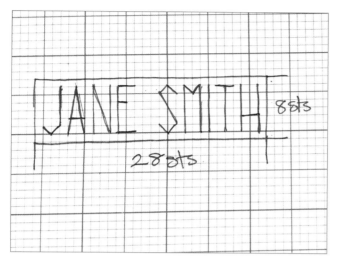
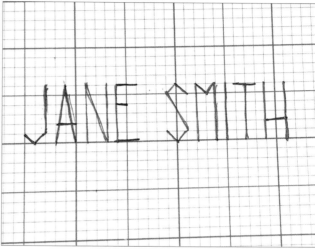

Once you have your name drawn out you will be able to see how much space it takes up, and you can centre it nicely within the space left on the chart for the name.

Then either copy it in the right place onto a photocopy of your chart, or if you are more confident, simply sew the name in the correct place on the design using your hand drawn chart.

Once you get used to and confident with changing colours and elements of bought charts, you'll see how easy it is to personalise designs to make them special to you and your family and it will open up a whole new area for you to explore in cross stitching.

DESIGNING A SAMPLER FROM MOTIFS

A traditional sampler will usually contain various elements, a border around the design, an alphabet and a selection of motifs all arranged together, which may also be within a small border of their own. A more modern sampler however can simply be a collection of motifs, usually themed that you have arranged together in an attractive manner to make a larger design. The simplest and most basic way to do this is with a set of four or six card sized charts put together into a single picture, so we'll look at how to go about doing this first.

ARRANGING SMALL CHARTS TOGETHER TO MAKE A LARGER DESIGN

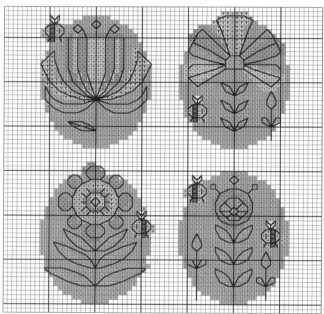

Once you have your set of charts, you will see these are very often all the same size and shape.

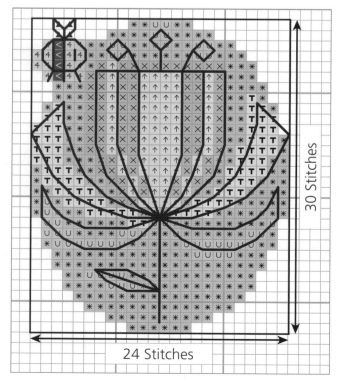

The first thing you need to decide is how you want to arrange them, they could be arranged into a square, horizontally or vertically, it's up to you and the look you wish to achieve. For this example we will arrange the designs into a square shape. If your designs don't have a regular border shape, first you will need to draw that on, and count how many squares each one takes up.

54

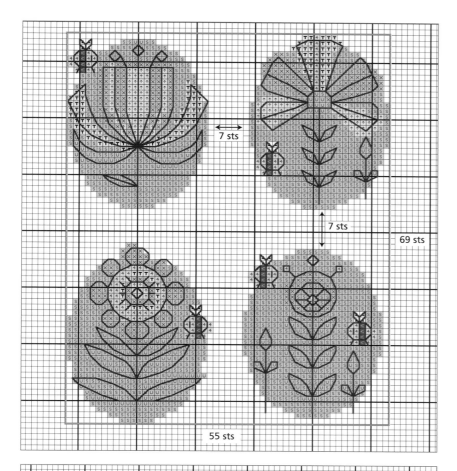

7 sts

7 sts

69 sts

55 sts

Now you can plan these shapes onto a piece of graph paper, leaving a small space between each one. Seven stitches is usually adequate. This will allow you to easily see and count how many stitches the arranged design takes up, and so work out how much fabric you will need to sew the designs together.

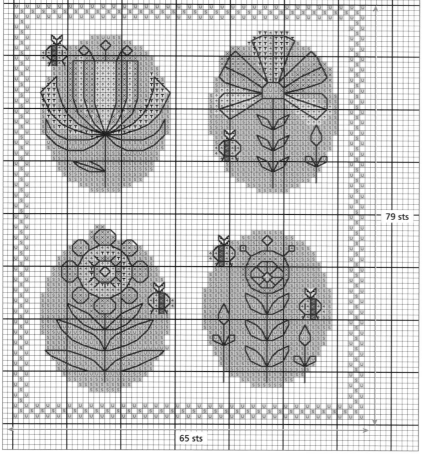

79 sts

65 sts

You could however decide to add more onto this design, either with a border all the way around the four charts or a small border around each one, you could even add on wording or other small motifs, it's really up to you. Now is the time to do this. Plan it all out by drawing as much or as little as you like onto the graph paper, and then once you are happy with how it looks, count up the total number of squares on your graph paper, to work out the number of stitches in the design and so find out how much fabric the design would use to complete it.

ARRANGING A SAMPLER FROM MOTIFS

Another slightly more daunting way to put together a sampler is from small motifs which you might find in a design library or book. These are often themed, with a selection of different sized motifs and borders, so this needs to be approached a little differently.

Once you have found the motifs you would like to work with, the first thing to do is to photocopy them all so you can cut them out. Try to get the grid sizes of the motifs all the same size and also the same size as the graph paper you have to arrange them on by adjusting them as you photocopy them. If you can't do this, and the motifs are quite simple you could copy them straight onto your graph paper to cut them out.

Next you need to decide what size you would like your finished sampler to be. This can just be a rough guide at this stage, it may change by a stitch or two in either direction once you plan in your designs, but it's good to have a guide size in mind.

Start by placing your border, if you have decided to use one. These are often provided as a repeat motif, so you can simply copy the design onto the graph paper in your chosen colours using coloured pencils or pens.

Now it's time to arrange your motifs, you could have a larger central image with smaller ones around the outside, have the motifs simply arranged randomly in a pleasing fashion or have the motifs arranged more regimentally so you can add borders around individual ones. It's really up to you. As the motifs are on cut out paper, you are free to move them around as much as you like inside the main chart area until you are happy with the result.

Once you find an arrangement you like, glue the motifs in place onto the main grid, being careful to line up the grid lines. Or if you prefer to you could copy each motif onto the main grid using coloured pens or pencils. This has the advantage of allowing you to change the colours of the original motif designs if you should wish to.

Now you have your finished chart to work from and a sampler that is unique to yourself.

DESIGNING YOUR OWN CHART

Once you have become confident with creating a design from existing motifs and borders or personalising an existing chart, you may wish to give designing your own chart from scratch a go.

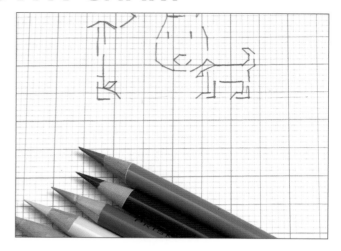

There are a number of ways you could do this. You could convert a photo of a scene, family member or pet, draw designs on paper by hand or use computer software to chart your design. It really depends on how much you wish to spend or how often you think you would like to design your own chart. Hand drawing charts onto a gridded paper is the easiest and most cost efficient way to start as you need no real specialist equipment, so we'll look at that method first.

DRAWING A CHART ON GRIDDED PAPER

To start you will need a drawing of what it is you wish to chart. It can be quite simple, just showing the main outline shapes. You can either draw this freehand or you could trace a photograph that you have taken. For this example I'll show you how to chart a little butterfly sketch that I drew freehand.

Next you will need to decide how big you want the finished stitching to be and work out how big that is in stitches, or squares on your gridded paper. You can buy special gridded paper that is a specific stitch count, but it's not necessary, basic stationary graph paper will be fine. You just have to remember that the finished stitched size won't be the same as the size you see when you are drawing the design or the chart.

So if we want our butterfly to be 7.3 cm x 5.5 cm on 14 count aida. Then we can work out that it would need to be 40 x 30 stitches or squares big on the graph paper. We get this number by dividing the amount in centimetres by 2.54 to convert the measurement to inches and then multiply that number by 14 (or whatever the count of the fabric is that you wish to work on) to arrive at the stitch amount.

If the drawing of the butterfly needs to change to fit this size now is the time to do it, you could use a photocopier to adjust the size up or down, or you could simply just re-draw it to the correct size. Once you have the drawing to the correct size you can colour it if you wish using coloured pencils or pens, just to give you an idea of what colours you wish to use on the design, where they go, how they interact with each other and how the finished design will look.

Now you need to trace the main outline and key points of the butterfly and transfer it onto the graph paper. Taking care to line the drawing up with the grid and to keep it square.

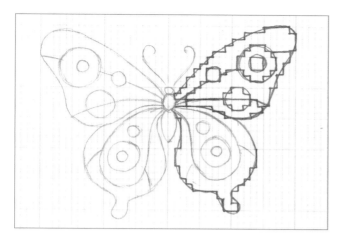
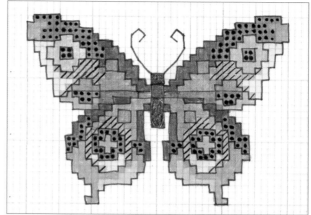

Draw over the design that you have transferred to the graph paper sticking to the squares on the paper, choose the squares that are the closest match the sketch outline. It's best to do this in pencil to start with, so you can adjust the lines if they don't work or appear how you want them to look the first time. It can sometimes take a little bit of trial and error to make the elements balance, look correct and how you would like. When you are happy with the outlines you have drawn you can, if you wish, go over them using a fine liner pen to help them stand out and make it easier for you to see them.

To add colour to your chart it's simply a matter of colouring in the squares. Each square represents a stitch, so be careful to follow the grid when you colour. If some of your colours are very close in tone where you have added shading for instance, then you can add simple symbols over these with a black fine liner pen. If you are adding any back stitch to the design this can also be added again being careful to stick to the grid structure of the graph paper.

The last thing you need to do to finish your chart and make it into something you can sew from is to add on a key and any other information you need to know about it such as a chart size and centre marks. To make the key copy all the different colour squares you have used down the side or underneath your chart, then using your threads or shade card look at the colours you need and match them to threads, writing down the skein numbers next to the coloured squares to create the key.

Your chart is now finished and you are ready to stitch.

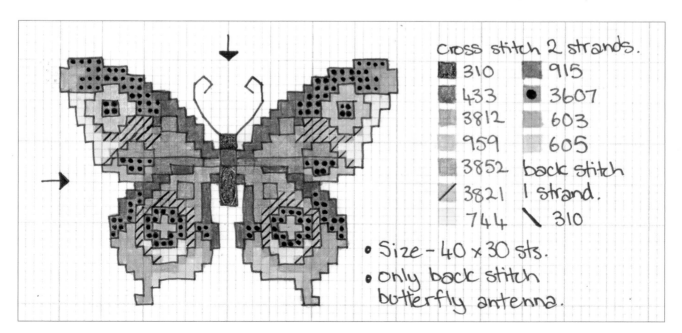

Cross stitch 2 strands.
310   915
433   3607
3812   603
959   605
3852   back stitch
3821   1 strand.
744   310

• Size – 40 x 30 sts.
• Only back stitch butterfly antenna.

DRAWING A CHART ON DIGITAL GRIDDED PAPER

Rather than designing a chart on paper with pencils and pens you can also now buy apps that will allow you to chart a design onto a computer or tablet, even your phone.

If you are familiar with vector drawing software and already own this then it is simply a matter of drawing a grid of lots and lots of small squares that you can colour in, which sounds tedious, but once you have a master document set up you can use it over and over again. Or with a little patient you can draw a chart using software such as excel or numbers. They would of course just be charts made up of coloured blocks rather than symbols, so they would need to be fairly simple if you intended to sew from them.

You do however have the advantage of being able to choose as many different colours to work with as you like though and as it's digital drawing you can also change colours very easily or erase sections, which is something that you can't easily do on traditional gridded paper.

If you want to give drawing on a digital gridded paper a go but don't yet feel ready for a cross stitch software package, then it's well worth searching on your app store for graph paper apps. One I've found that works well for drawing basic charts is GridMaker.

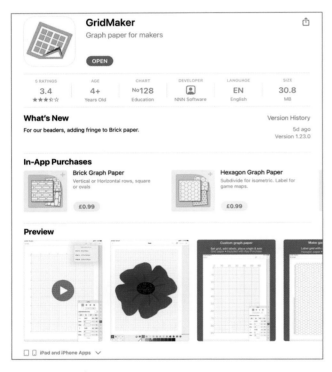

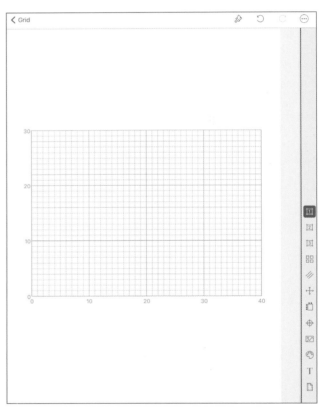

Using this app you can draw a grid quickly and easily to whatever size you wish, you can number the axis, mark in the centre, drop in an image to trace behind the grid and then switch it to a drawing mode to allow you to draw the chart.

To start you first need the image that you wish to convert into a chart. I'll use the little butterfly sketch that I used before when we looked at charting on traditional gridded paper.

Once you have the GridMaker app installed on your iPad or iPhone, you need to set up the grid size that you want to use by clicking on the icons down the right hand side of the screen and typing in your requirements. You can also choose the colour of the grid, if it has numbers, or a centre mark here too, as well as various other things so it's worth spending a little time playing with these options to find out how you want the grid to be set.

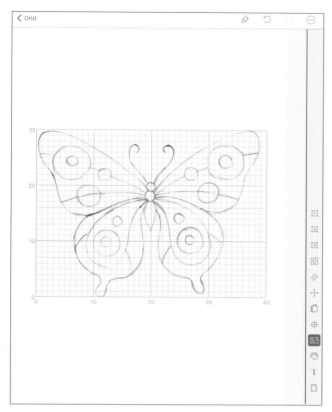

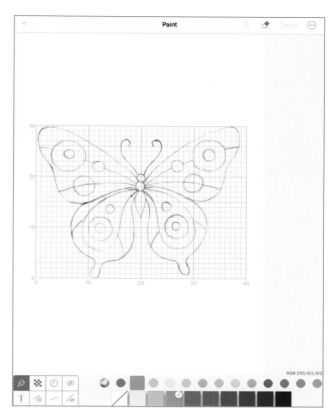

Once you have the grid just how you'd like it, click on the icon that looks like a little landscape on the right hand side, this allows you to choose the image you want to place behind the grid to trace.

Now you're ready to switch the app to painting mode, by clicking on the little paint brush icon at the top of the screen, this will change the tools that you can see to the ones shown above.

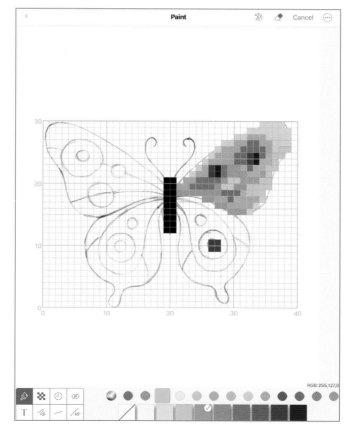

To colour the squares in choose the paint brush tool and a colour then simply click the square you wish to be that colour to fill it in. Continue doing this with the different colours until you have all the cross stitch filled in are happy with how it looks.

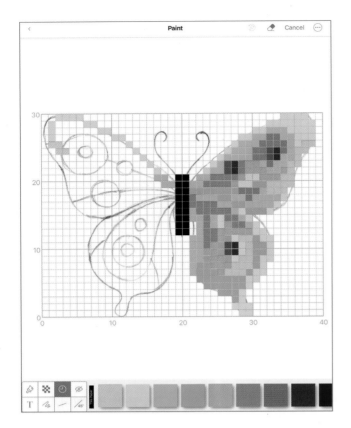

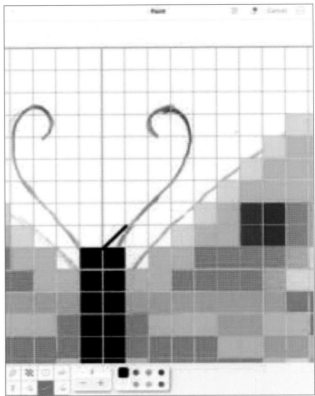

If you want to delete parts of the design, you can do this by selecting the swatch on the colours with the red line through, this will put the square back to no colour, or you could of course just change the colour of a square by clicking on it with a new colour.

Unfortunately though, like with traditional graph paper there is no function to select and duplicate areas, so to repeat the wings to the other side you will need to draw them in by hand.

You can however hide the sketch if it is in the way. If you click on the eye icon you will see you can hide and unhide various elements within the drawing.

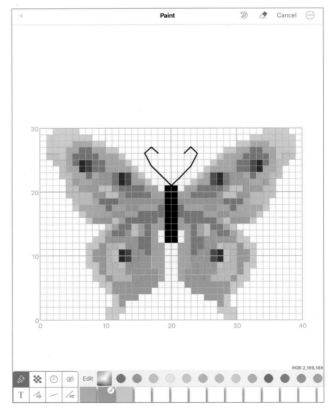

Once you have drawn in the cross stitches then you can add the back stitch if there is any by switching to one of the line tools and choosing a colour to draw with and complete your design.

Much like when you draw a chart onto paper with pencils, the colours used here aren't thread colours, and the software won't output any sort of key, so I find it beneficial to colour in squares on the chart with every colour that you have used in the design.

The software does have a typing tool, so if you know the thread numbers that the colours refer to you could type these in, or you can simply print it as it is and then write in the thread colours next to the colour blocks to make a key once you have looked at your threads and chosen the ones you'd most like to use.

To output the design you just need to click on the three dots at the top and choose the option you want, either a pdf, image or to print it and you will have a chart that you can then use to sew a design from.

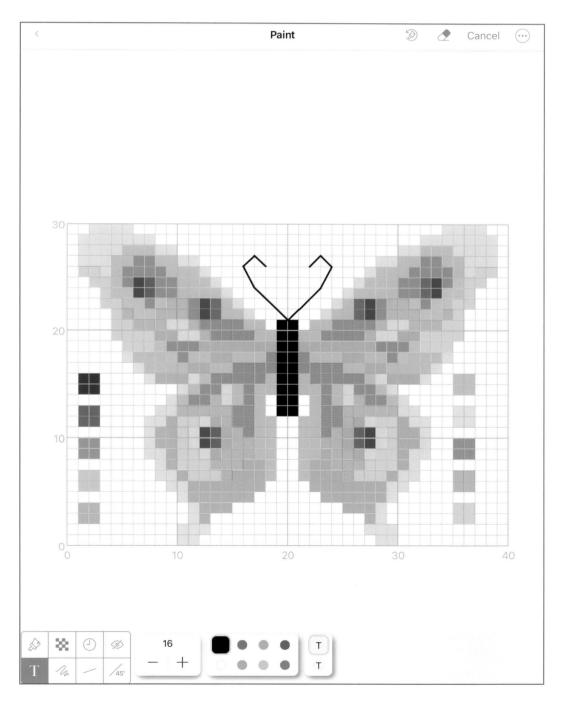

LOOKING AT CROSS STITCH SOFTWARES

THE BENEFITS

Once you have a feel for designing charts by hand onto gridded paper, and if you feel you would like to advance and do cross stitch design regularly, then it's probably time to look into buying some computer software.

Designing charts on a computer has certain advantages over drawing charts by hand, the main one being it reduces the time taken to draw a chart and allows you to produce more complex charts that are easily legible, so a computer can be a very useful tool to aid you in designing your charts.

An Undo Button

Firstly the computer software has an undo button, so you can easily go backwards to the point where you want to change the design without having to rub out and redraw large sections of a design, this is particularly useful if it's a very detailed area of the chart, or it is taking you some time to get it just right, computers unlike gridded paper doesn't wear through and become unreadable with time and over use.

Changing Colours

You can easily change colours of an object, if you coloured a section of a hand drawn design in a colour that then didn't work out how you thought, you'd have to paste a new piece of paper over that section and draw the whole thing again, not so with a computer, you can easily change either everything in a certain skein colour, or just repaint a small section of the design into a different colour, allowing you much more freedom and the ability to quickly see different colour options.

Repositioning an Object

Moving around objects or parts of a design becomes much easier when you are using a computer, if something isn't quite centred, or you just wish to move it to a different part of the design, then just select all the object and move it to the correct position, there's no need to redraw anything. The computer will move the back stitch, cross stitch and everything else in the selection.

Repeating and Mirroring Objects

The computer can copy and paste sections, as well as rotate and mirror them, so repeat borders and symmetrical designs become much easier, there's no need to spend ages working it all out by hand, redrawing and colouring sections over and over again.

There are of course many advantages to designing on a computer, and you'll discover them for yourself and learn the features you want to use most often, but I'll go over some of the main ones here.

Adding Complexity

On the computer you can easily draw in fractional stitches and half cross stitches and see what they would look like, also you can choose to use a different number of strands of thread for different parts of the design, making a chart as complicated or as simple as you wish. Some software will even have special stitches built in, so you can easily draw eyelets and other stitches with just one click of the mouse.

Adding Symbols

All cross stitch software will add symbols to the chart if you ask it to, which can be invaluable when you have chosen three or four shades of thread that are very similar. You can produce much more delicate and realistic looking charts and make them easy for another person to understand them and be able to sew from them.

Viewing the Design

You will have all the thread colours within various manufacturers libraries at your finger tips, there's no need to simply make do with a green coloured pencil that is nearly the right shade and match it to the thread later, the software has the colours built in, so you can see your design on screen very close to how it would appear when sewn.

Many of the cross stitch software even allows you to see on screen what the designs would look like on the fabric with a stitched simulated view, which can be extremely useful to give you a quick idea of what the design would look like on different coloured fabrics.

WHICH SOFTWARE TO CHOOSE?

Which software is best for you of course very much depends on your needs, and how often you will use the software and so determines how much you wish to spend, also you should take your computer and it's operating system into account, you need software that will work efficiently with your own set up.

There are many, many different manufacturer's of cross stitch software, and we are fortunate nowadays that many of them have websites that we can look at before purchasing, often they also offer a demo version of the software too, so you can download the software and use it before you buy. You usually can't save or export the design, but you will at least be able to see and try it's particular features before you buy it to see if it is suitable. Over the years I have tried out many of them, some I found to be better than others but they do usually offer similar features within them, so

it can simply be a matter of personal preference for how the different softwares are laid out on the screen or how they handle on your computer that determines which you prefer. So while reviews and guides are a good place to start I would very much recommend that you spend a little time downloading and trying as many of them as you can before you settle on one in particular.

Some of the more popular and established ones you could look at include:

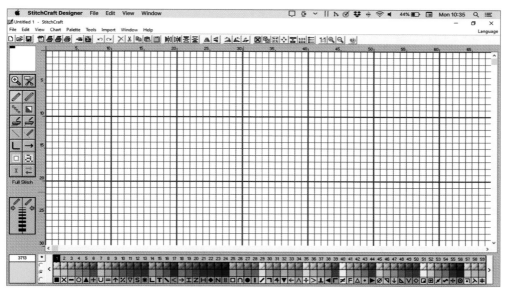

STITCHCRAFT DESIGNER

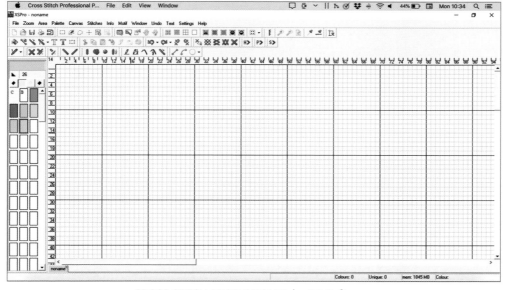

CROSS STITCH PROFESSIONAL by DP Software

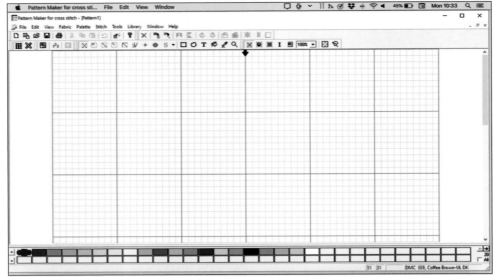

PATTERN MAKER

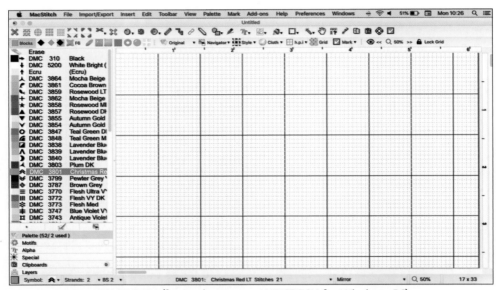

MACSTITCH (for Apple Macs or WINSTITCH for Windows PC)

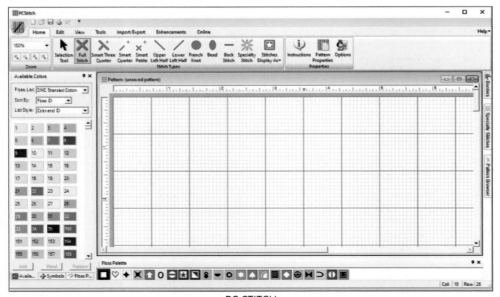

PC STITCH

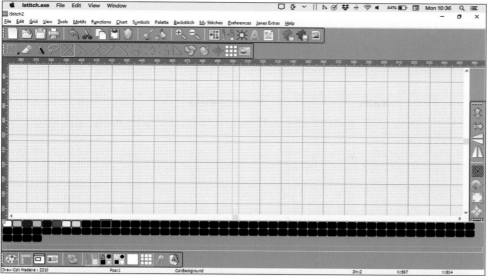

JANE GREENOFF'S ISTITCH

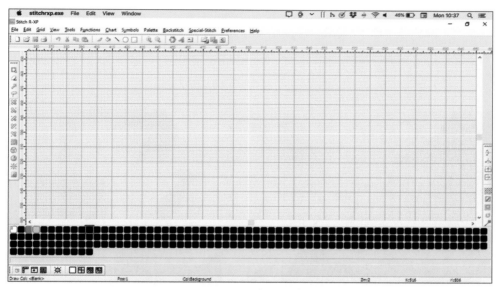

STITCH R-XP by ILSoft

All of these programmes do a similar job, often the places you will find differences in them is in the more advanced features such as their ability to handle fractional and special stitches, view stitches and fabrics and their chart output options.

I myself use four different cross stitch programmes regularly, which I use when is usually determined by who it is I'm working for, if I send a cross stitch chart to another company it is much more convenient for them if they have software that can open the chart I sent to them. The four programmes I use in my daily work are StitchCraft, Cross Stitch Professional, Pattern Maker and PC Stitch. However the charts in this book were designed using StitchCraft, so when I talk about building charts in software later it will be that particular software we will be looking at.

CONVERTING A PHOTOGRAPH TO A CROSS STITCH CHART

There are a few companies that will take your photo and convert it into a cross stitch pattern for you, but if you have bought cross stitch software, then with a little experimentation you should be able to produce your own with no trouble at all.

Before you start you need to consider a few things, the first being the actual photograph that you are using. Is it a good quality picture, the software can only translate what you give it to translate, so if the photo looks a little dark, or lacking in contrast, then that should be taken care of first with some photo correcting software. Also it should be a high resolution and not be pixelated, unless of course that's the look you want.

You need to consider the size of your design. The more stitches it will have then the more detail the software can fit into the space, but of course the more time, fabric and thread it will take to stitch it, so this needs to be considered too.

Finally there is the amount of colours you want to use to sew the design to consider. The more colours the design uses the closer it will be to the original, but again this adds cost to your sewing, so having 100 different skein colours might not be the best option. It's often best to try a photo conversion of the same picture with different colour amounts set. You could start by setting the maximum colours to 25, then try 50 and so on, to see which result you prefer.

For this example of a photo conversion I'm going to use the flower photograph below, and StitchCraft software.

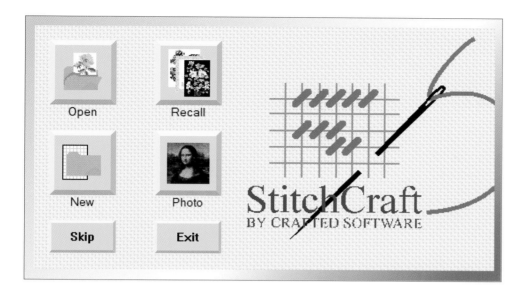

To start open the Stitch Craft software and click on the button which says "photo"

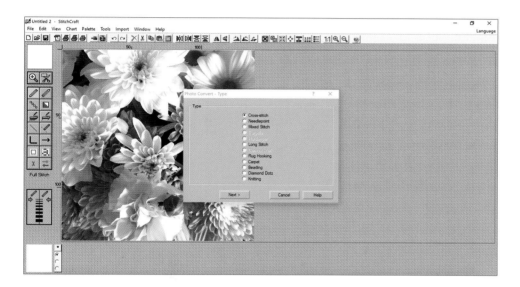

Once you have told the software where it can find the photograph you want to convert then you will see a dialogue box with various options for what kind of chart you want to create, click the cross stitch option on in this box.

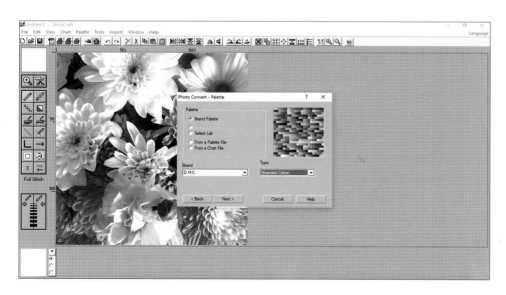

Now on the next dialogue box click on the brand palette option, and choose which particular brand and type of threads you would like to use in your sewing, I've chosen to use DMC stranded cotton.

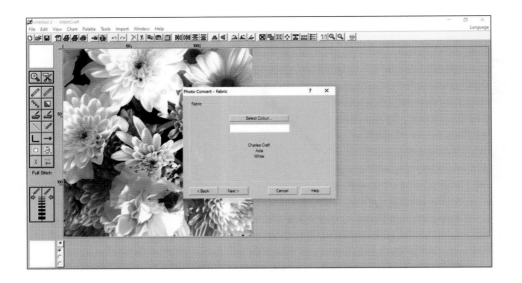

Next it's fabric and you need to tell the software what kind of fabric you wish to use. For this example I've set it to white aida as the design is a full cover piece and the fabric won't be seen anyway.

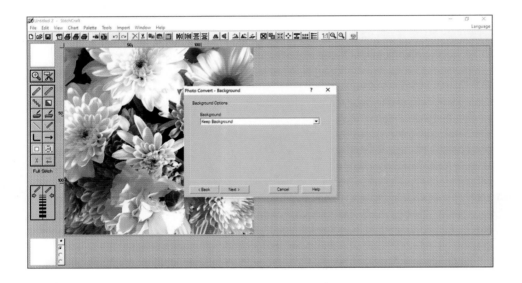

The next setting asks you if you want to remove the white background or the black background, which can be useful if the picture you have is an object on an empty background that you don't want to stitch. As this is a full cover piece I've set it to the "Keep Background" option.

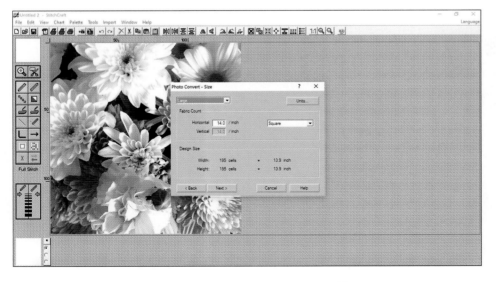

After you have chosen what style and colour of fabric to use, you need to tell the software what fabric count the fabric is, and also how big you wish the design to be. StitchCraft has some preset sizes, but you can also set it to a custom size and type in whatever you wish. I've set it to large, which is 195 x 195 stitches.

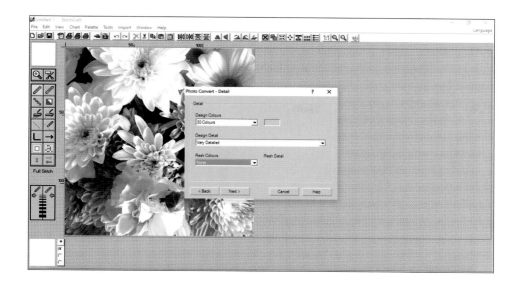

We can now start to choose how many colours the design should have and how detailed you wish it to be. This is the part where you have more control over how to change the look of the final chart.

For this example I used 30 colours from the drop down menu, and also set the detail to very as I wanted to try to keep as much definition in the flowers as possible. The flesh colours option I left set to none, but if your photo does contain people then you would set this to whatever the skin tone is of the people in the photo to help the software determine which colours to use in the chart.

As you can see the resulting chart is quite detailed but perhaps a little more muted than the original photograph, as the software has had to make some of the colours an average between the light and the dark extremes in the photo.

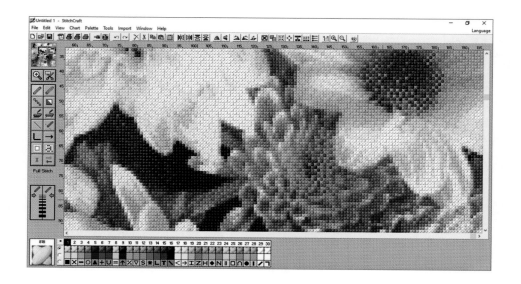

However the design is quite pleasing and when we zoom in we can see there is lots of detail present in the chart, so if you are happy with this first result then it's simply a matter of saving and exporting the design so you can sew your design from it.

If you aren't happy with how the chart turned out and would like to try different settings to convert your photo, then you simply have to go up to the import button at the top and go down to redo photo, there is no need to start again from the beginning of the process.

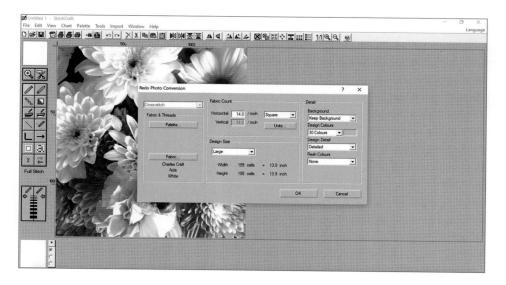

This will bring up a dialogue box as you can see opposite, and you can change the settings to achieve a different outcome.

Just to show you what difference using a large amount of thread colours makes, I changed the colours to be set at 100, and the design detail to be set at very detailed again.

Now the design has much more colour and isn't so muted, the software can pick up small differences in shades and tones.

But of course it is your photo conversion, so you can try different settings as many times as you like until your are happy and have a design that uses the number of colours you wish to use.

For a contrast and just to show you how different a photograph can look with different settings, here I converted the exact same photograph as before, I left the design size and the thread manufacturer's palette the same but this time I set the design colours to 10 and the design detail to blocky.

As you can see the result is very different, very muted and almost monotone as the software tried to make sense of a complex photo with so few colours to work with. It's also made it much more printed looking rather than looking like a photograph it has taken on a pattern quality, which does have a certain appeal and could be a good starting point to change the thread colours in the palette and create a very unique design.

Below I've converted the exact same photograph into some of the software programmes that I use, so you can see a comparison of how the different software handles the same photograph. For the most part I left the settings as the default setting, but I did change the size of the finished design and also the amount of colours used in each conversion.

The settings were set each time to make a chart that was 195 x 195 stitches, using DMC stranded cotton and 30 shades.

Converted using
StitchCraft software

Converted using
Cross Stitch Professional software

Converted using
Pattern Maker software

DESIGNING A CHART USING CROSS STITCH SOFTWARE

Although using your cross stitch software to convert a photograph that you own can be very rewarding and will provide you lots of unique and personal things to sew, you may wish to use the software to design a chart for yourself from scratch to chart a drawing you have done or create a custom piece that is unique.

In this section I'll look at how to go about this, using the butterfly drawing that I used earlier and StitchCraft software. Of course all software will look slightly different, the tools will have different icons and be in different places, but the process will be the same and if you consult your particular software manual or the help section within the software you'll soon become familiar with your tools and where to find them.

To start you need to scan your drawing into your computer and crop it down to a rectangle so that you just have the drawing without the surrounding blank paper. You may also find it useful to lighten it up slightly too, so that when it is dropped into the software it is just a faint image in the background and you can draw over it easily.

Once you have opened a new blank document in your software the next step is to import your drawing, but this time you need to import it as an image you can trace over rather than ask the software to convert it to a chart. As you import the image you would also tell the software how big the design is to be, I've set mine to 40 x 30 stitches as it was before in the hand drawn chart example.

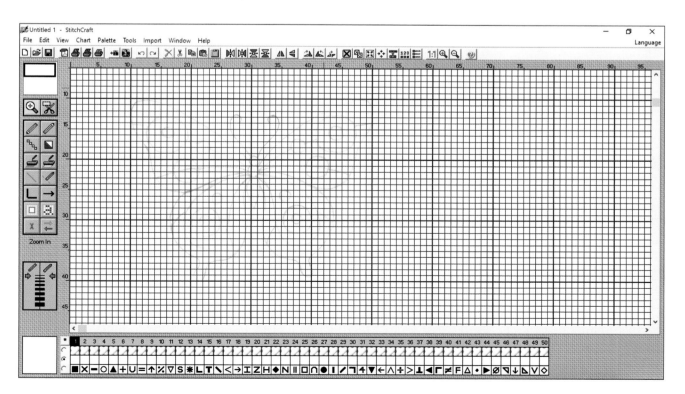

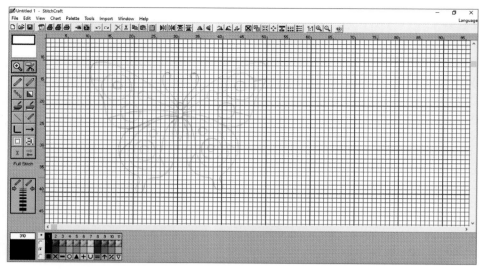

If you know which colours you wish to use in the design then you can tell the software what those are now. Or you could simply choose and add colours as you go.

I'm using the same colours as in the previous example so I've allocated these in my colour swatches.

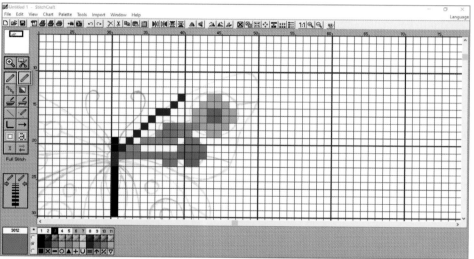

Now choosing your whole cross stitch tool, choose a colour and begin to fill in the squares, keeping as close to the drawn outline as you can. As you can see I'm just drawing half of the design as it is a symmetrical one and we can copy and paste in the other half.

Finish colouring in all the squares to complete the right side of the butterfly, then choosing your back stitch tool and the black thread you can draw in the antenna, but again only one side.

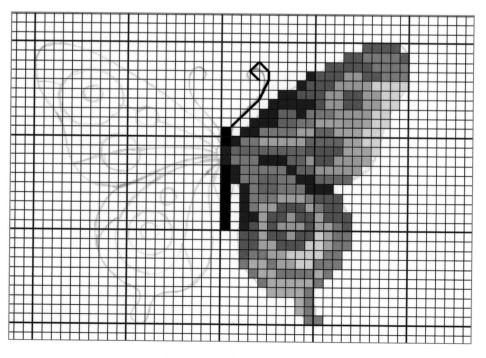

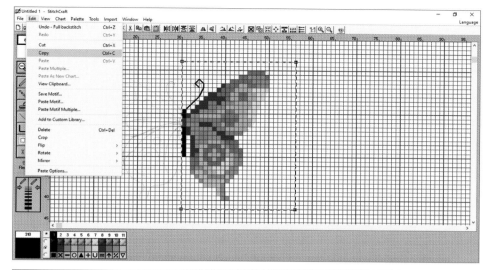

Once you are happy with how the right hand side of the butterfly looks then using your selection tool draw around the butterfly to select it and ask the software to copy and then paste the selection.

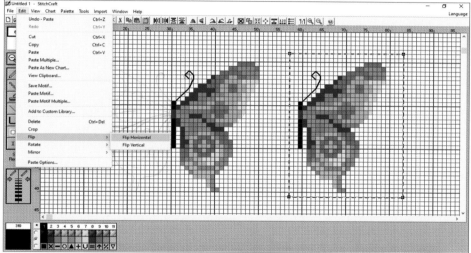

Copying and pasting the selection will duplicate it exactly for you, now you simply have to ask it to flip the selection so you have the left half of the butterfly.

The flip command is often located under the edit tab in the software, but many have short cut buttons as well, so it can be helpful to learn these too, this will allow you to carry out operations with just a simple click of your mouse.

Position your newly flipped wing in the correct place then delete the sketch that you imported to trace over.

Your butterfly design is now complete and is ready to be output as a chart.

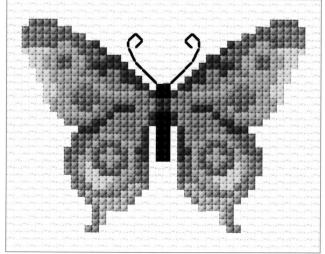

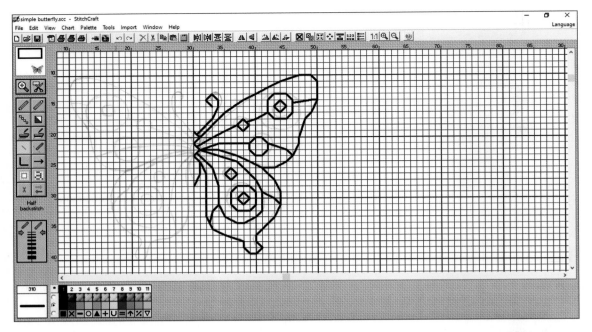

If you wish to draw a chart that is a little more complex or contains more back stitch than just the butterfly antenna, then we go about this in much the same way as before, the main difference is that you need to draw in all the back stitch first, as the imported drawing becomes covered once you start to colour in the squares.

Using your back stitch tool and selecting the thread colour you wish to use you can draw over the pencil lines, try to keep as close to them as you can, as you did before when you filled in the squares with whole cross stitch, and again only drawing the right hand side as we will copy, paste and flip it later.

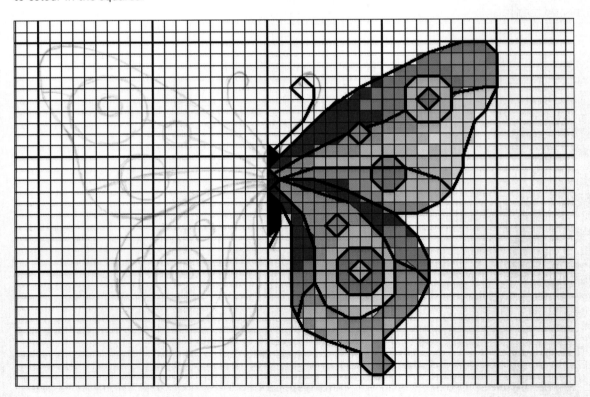

Once you are happy with the back stitch lines then you simply colour in the squares as you did before, you may decide as I did here to add in some fractional stitches to keep closer to the line, do this by selecting your fractional stitch tool rather than the whole cross stitch tool.

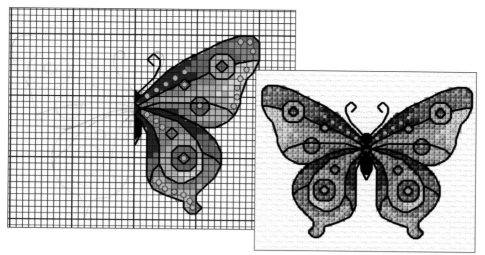

If you want to add in any French knots then you can do this after you have finished filling in all the cross stitch by selecting your French knot tool and the colour you wish them to be.

Copy, paste and flip the wings as you did before to create the left hand side of the butterfly and complete your design.

If you wish to change the colours within your drawn design maybe because one of them doesn't look quite right, or you just want to see how it would look with a different colour scheme, this is very easy to do. On most software if you double click the colour swatch you want to change, it will bring up the colour palette, then it's simply a matter of choosing a new colour for that swatch.

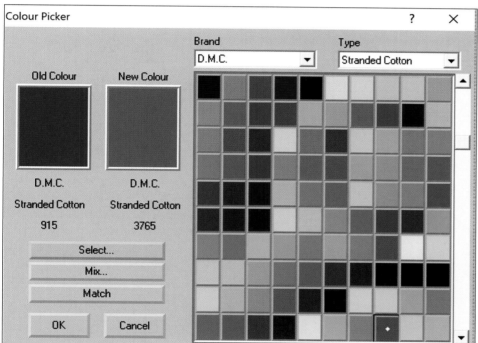

When you click ok and go back to your chart you will see that all the stitches in that colour over the whole of the design has changed. If you wish to just change a section then there is usually a bucket looking tool which will flood fill an area to save you from clicking on individual stitches to change them, which is handy if it is a large section.

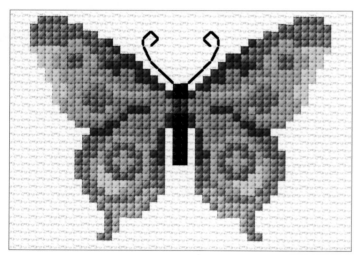

You could change just one colour, to correct a shade or how it sits against another colour, or you could change them all, which can change the look of the design completely and provide you with a new and different chart to sew.

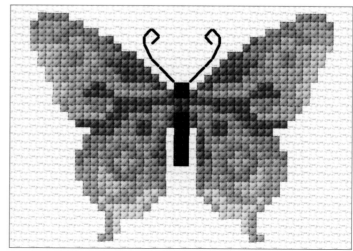

As you can see, changing all the colours to different ones can be quite effective, you could just keep swapping the colours, saving as you go to create a whole set of different coloured butterflies to sew.

Or you could start to combine them into a larger design, even just a very simple use of the copy, paste, flip and rotate tools can give some very rewarding results, especially if you add in a few extra simple complementary motifs, the possibilities are endless once you start to experiment with your software and use your imagination.

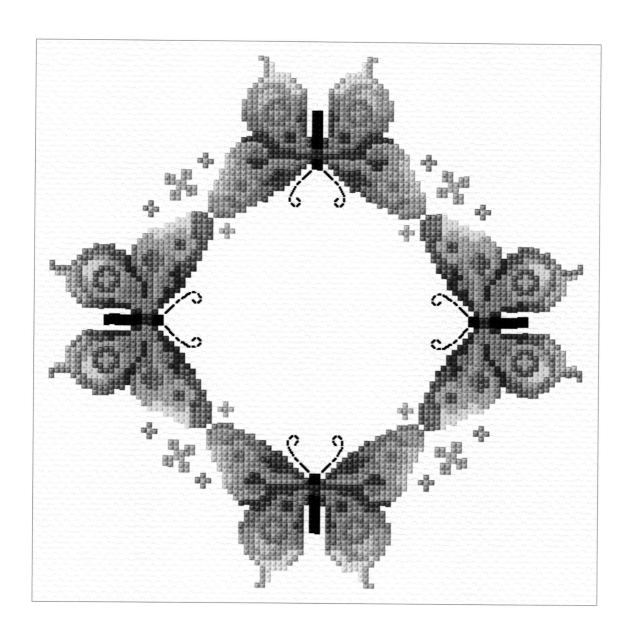

EXPORTING YOUR CHART

Once you have designed your chart and finished it just how you want it to look, you will need to export it to sew from, most usually the software will export the design and make it into a PDF format so you can open it without needing the original cross stitch software.

Before you do export the chart however it's a good idea to look at various elements of the chart and make sure you have it ready to be output. First you need to make sure the chart grid size is the same size as the design size. If you have been working on a larger canvas than the design actually is, as I often do to allow extra space around the design to manipulate elements, then when you have finished you need to crop the chart down to the size of the design. When I'm using StitchCraft then I usually crop it down but allow a 3 square border all around, this is to allow space to add on the centre mark arrows. Some software will print these outside the chart boundaries, so you need to work out what works best for the software you are using and also how you want the chart to look.

Once you've cropped the chart down, you need to remove any colours of thread that you haven't used, the software will usually do this for you automatically when you ask it to remove any unused colours and duplicates, then it's time to have a look at the symbols that the design is using for each colour. They may look alright, but if not then the ones that don't work need to be changed to others so the chart is more legible. Again how this is done can differ from one programme to another, sometimes there is a section in the drop down menu for changing symbols, and sometimes it's simply a matter of double clicking, or right clicking the colour in the palette to bring up the symbol library.

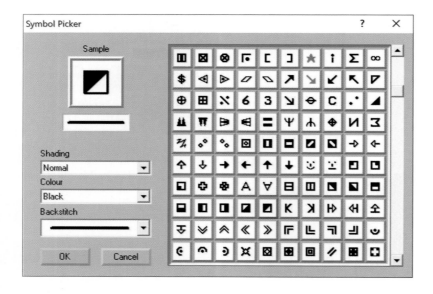

Different software manufacturers build different symbol fonts into their software, so you need to get to know the symbols that are on offer in your particular software so you will know which symbols print better, or view better or just look better on certain colours.

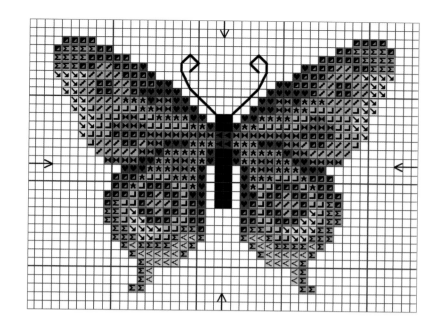

Once you have chosen the symbols you like best then you can switch the view on screen to show you how those symbols would appear on your chart when it is turned into a pdf, if there are any that don't work, or you notice two that sit close together and look too similar, then go back and change them until you have a chart in which the symbols work and are legible.

Now it's time to export the design. You can print charts in all sorts of ways depending on what your software allows. You might be able to add on notes, add numbers to the grid, vary the look of the grid, add page overlaps or add a key to each page, So you need to explore your particular software and decide which functions you want to use when you print your charts.

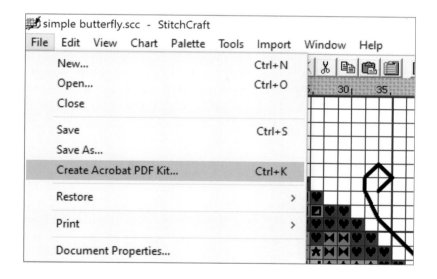

The export function is usually located under the file tab at the top of the screen. In my software it is called Create Acrobat PDF Kit, but it could also say export graphic or export pdf.

Click on this option and then you need to go through the menus that will pop up tell the software how you want to output the chart.

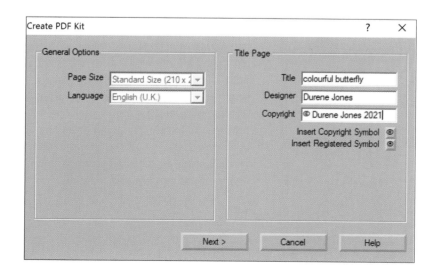

If you wish to you can give the pdf a title and also add on your name or a company name and also a copyright. This information will be printed onto the cover page of the chart pdf.

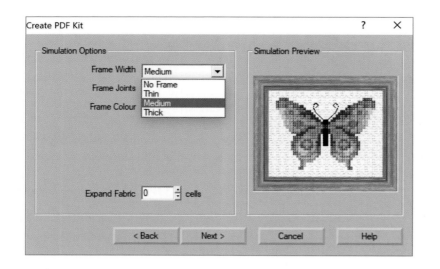

You can add a stitched simulation to the cover page of the pdf. Even if you are just designing charts for your own personal use, this is a useful feature as it allows you to quickly identify what the design is. You can usually choose different looks to this stitched simulation. You could choose to have it with no frame at all or a frame with different thicknesses.

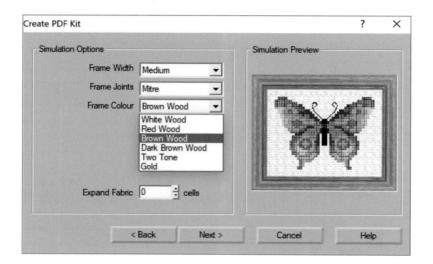

You can also choose to have the frame in different colours.

Whilst this particular software doesn't have a frame mount option, some do so you could also choose to have your sewing shown with different coloured mounts when they are in the framed view.

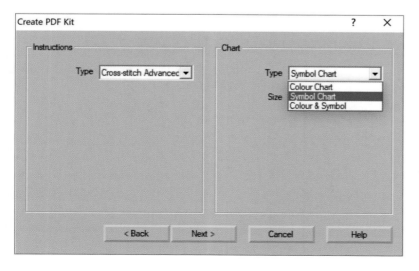

Then it's onto deciding how you would like the actual chart to print. Most software will have the option to print the symbol onto a coloured block. Or the option to print black symbols on a white background. But many have other options too, such as printing coloured tints behind symbols or even coloured symbols, so it's well worth trying various options and settings to find your personal preference.

Here are some examples of the chart output options you might see in your software.

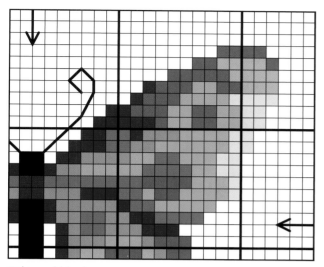

Coloured blocks

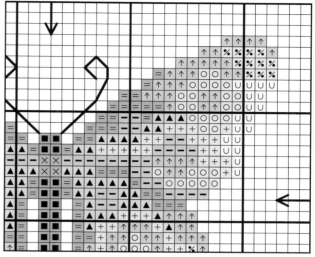

Tinted coloured blocks with symbols

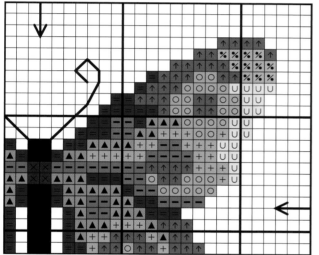

Coloured blocks with symbols

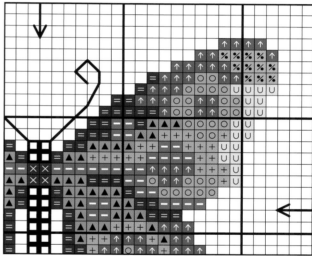

Coloured blocks with black symbols on light colours and white symbols on dark colours

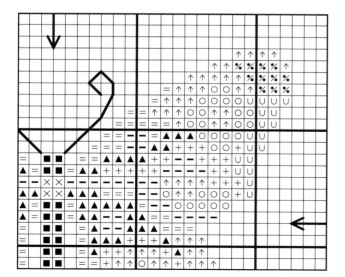

Black and white symbols

When you export the chart using these various output options the key will also change to suit the chart, so that you can easily identify which symbols are to be sewn in which thread colours.

Key

Colour	Symbol	Backstitch	Cat. No.	Brand	Type	Stitches	Skeins
	■	———	310	D.M.C.	Stranded Cotton	32	0.1
	◄		433	D.M.C.	Stranded Cotton	4	0.1
	⋈		3812	D.M.C.	Stranded Cotton	60	0.1
	╱		959	D.M.C.	Stranded Cotton	68	0.1
	★		3852	D.M.C.	Stranded Cotton	66	0.1
	⌐		3821	D.M.C.	Stranded Cotton	80	0.1
	↘		744	D.M.C.	Stranded Cotton	52	0.1
	♥		915	D.M.C.	Stranded Cotton	70	0.1
	◪		3607	D.M.C.	Stranded Cotton	130	0.1
	Σ		603	D.M.C.	Stranded Cotton	76	0.1
	<		605	D.M.C.	Stranded Cotton	32	0.1

Example of a key output using the coloured blocks with both black and white symbols option.

Key

Colour	Symbol	Backstitch	Cat. No.	Brand	Type	Stitches	Skeins
	□	———	310	D.M.C.	Stranded Cotton	32	0.1
	◄		433	D.M.C.	Stranded Cotton	4	0.1
	⋈		3812	D.M.C.	Stranded Cotton	60	0.1
	╱		959	D.M.C.	Stranded Cotton	68	0.1
	★		3852	D.M.C.	Stranded Cotton	66	0.1
	⌐		3821	D.M.C.	Stranded Cotton	80	0.1
	↘		744	D.M.C.	Stranded Cotton	52	0.1
	♥		915	D.M.C.	Stranded Cotton	70	0.1
	◪		3607	D.M.C.	Stranded Cotton	130	0.1
	Σ		603	D.M.C.	Stranded Cotton	76	0.1
	<		605	D.M.C.	Stranded Cotton	32	0.1

Example of a key output using the coloured blocks and coloured blocks with symbols option.

Once you have set all the options within the export function, it's simply a matter of clicking ok, and the software will generate a pdf for you, automatically chopping larger designs into various pages so the symbols are legible when they are printed. Or of course you could simply view the file on a pdf reader, which has the advantage of allowing you to zoom in as much as you like.

Within the pdf that the software prints you should expect to see something like the pages shown here.

A Cover Sheet

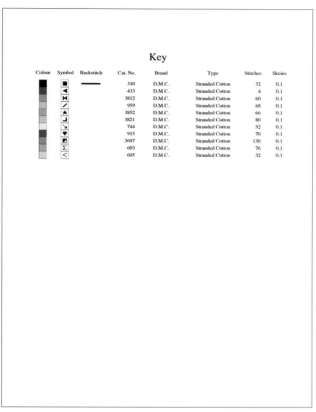

The Key

Information About the Chart

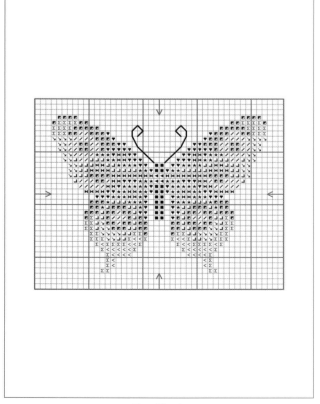

The Chart

CROSS STITCH DESIGN APPS

If you search cross stitch design on your app store, the likelihood is that you will mainly see painting by number style games, apps to help you view pdfs and track your progress, calculate fabric sizes or track your thread supplies. There isn't much in the way of good cross stitch software that I have found.

There are two apps that I've found which are used to design cross stitch charts from your own designs as well as being able to convert a photograph, those are Stitchly and StitchSketch, which unfortunately are currently only available on IOS.

As I write this Stitchly is still a relevantly new app, and so it's features are quite limited and basic, but the developers of the app seem to be responding to users comments and reviews and updating the app regularly, so it could be one to watch in the future to see how it progresses.

StitchSketch has the most features and is the one that I use if I want to design a small chart on my iPad, it offers

most of the features you would need when designing a chart, such as being able to drop a picture into the grid to trace, having a full thread colour list for various brands and being able to copy, paste and rotate an element. It is only really lacking in it's ability to simulate a stitched view and also the pdf output is limited to only colour or black and white, there are no special features to choose. But it is great for on the go designing or doing a bit of designing when I'm not in the mood to be sat in front of my computer any more that day. I can sit on the sofa watching a box set and still do a bit of designing or plan out parts of a larger design so I know how it will look when I chart it in my cross stitch software.

DESIGNING A CHART ON AN IPAD

For this demonstration I'll use the same butterfly sketch that I have used throughout this book, so you can see a direct comparison of how the chart looks charted in different ways.

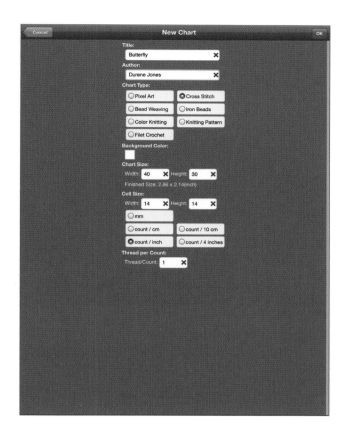
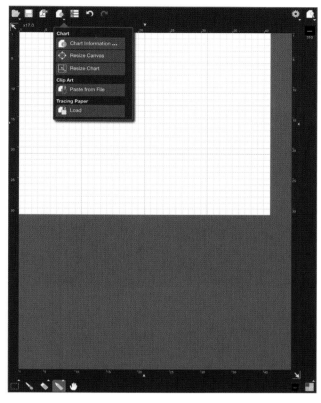

Once you have the StitchSketch app installed on your iPad or iPhone, it's simply a matter of clicking it to open it. It can look quite daunting the first few times you use it, and there can be quite a few different bits to learn, but practice will help, so don't be put off. Just experiment and play with the app and a small drawing or sketch and within no time you'll be feeling very comfortable with it.

Click on the New Chart option then you need to inform the software what it is you want to design, in this case it's cross stitch, so that needs to be clicked on.

You also need to enter the size that the chart should be and what count of fabric you want to use.

Next you need to import the sketch to trace from. Go up to the page icon at the top and go down to tracing paper, then choose the image you wish to trace from your photos. This command functions a little differently from desktop software in that, it will drop the image into the whole size of the chart and you can't scale it to a different size, so it's important that you had the chart set to the right size and not just random numbers.

Now it's time to start drawing. All of your tools are at the bottom of the screen, the drawing tools are stored under the pencil icon and when you press there you will see a pop up menu with lots of options, the main ones you will need are the pencil, for whole cross stitches and the line tool at the very top of the menu which is the back stitch tool. You can experiment with the others to see what they do, some of them are useful but I mainly use these two tools.

When you click on the back stitch icon, you will see it brings up an extra menu down the side that contains all the different stitches in a cross stitch design.

You could choose to use these tools to draw your chart, however it is worth remembering that the software can't produce a symbol view for the fractional stitches, they always remain as they look here, so you should experiment with that first and decide if you like how the finished chart looks and if you think you could sew the design from it.

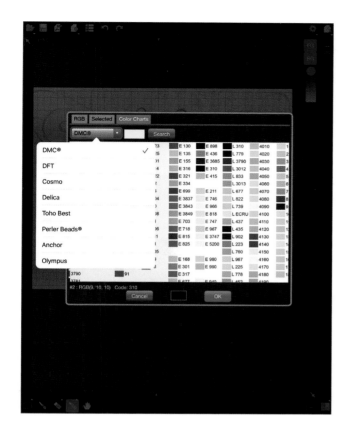

To choose the colours for the design click on the small colour swatch at the bottom right of the screen, mine shows a black colour swatch and this will bring up the colour menu where you can choose your colour brand and then the colours that you want to use.

Now you are all set to fill in the cross stitches, draw them in square by square keeping as close to the sketched outline as you can, but only drawing the right hand side as it's a symmetrical design and we can copy and paste the other wings later.

As with designing on a desktop computer if you want backstitch around the wings then you would need to draw these in first, so the sketch is not lost behind the cross stitches.

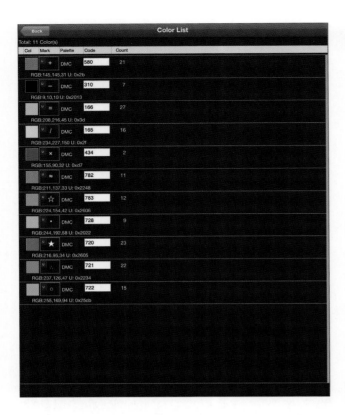

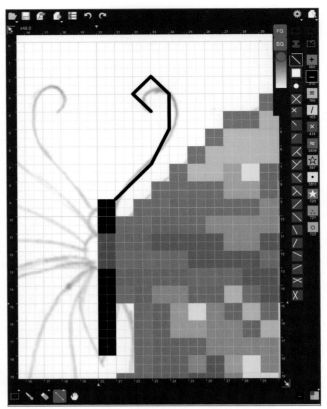

If you want to change some of the colours in your colour list because you don't like how they work together when you see them charted then that's a very simple process. You just have to click on the icon at the top of the screen that looks like a colour key, this will bring up all the information for the colours. You can then choose different colours by clicking on the swatch you want to change, or you can change the symbols by clicking on the symbol picture next to the colour swatch and control how the finished chart will look.

Now our right hand side of the butterfly is nearly finished, we just have to choose the back stitch tool and the colour we wish to use to draw on the back stitch.

When you do this the grid will change slightly to show you where the half way points of the squares are. The back stitch tool allows you to draw lines that anchor to either the grid or the half way points so you need to pay particular attention to where you are drawing if you want the back stitch to be simple and not piece aida blocks.

If you want to add French knots then you should also do that now using the tool that looks like a dot from this list of extra tools.

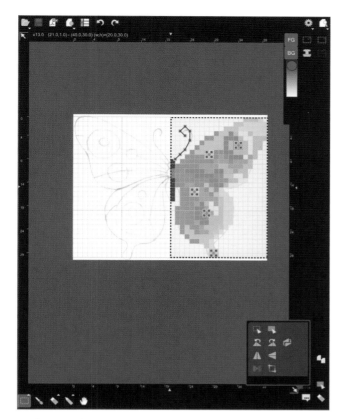
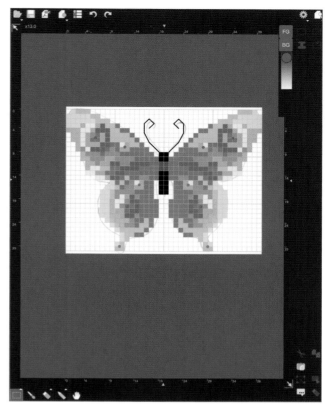

With the right hand side of the butterfly complete we need to copy it to make a left hand side.

First choose the selection tool in the bottom left hand corner or the screen and draw a box around the area you want to copy.

Next copy and paste the selection using the tools in the bottom right hand side of the screen The copy tool is the one that resembles two sheets of paper, and the paste one is the one that resembles a sheet of paper on a clipboard.

To flip the selection we need to click on the icon that looks like a square speech bubble to bring up some extra tools. Click on the flip horizontally tool and then move the selection into the correct position with the move tool at the very top right of this extra set of tools, the icon that resembles a greyed out selection and selection arrow.

The butterfly design is now complete and ready to be output as a PDF for sewing.

To output your chart first we need to click on the PDF icon at the top of the screen, this will bring up the generate pdf dialogue box.

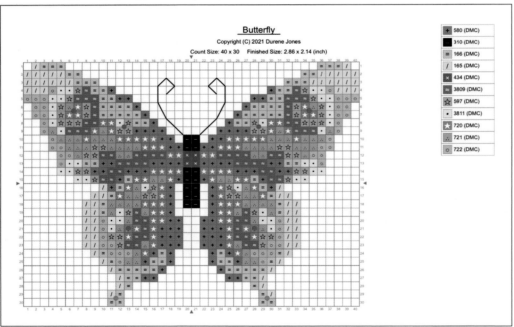

You can set this however you prefer your chart to look. The Mark button will output the design in black and white symbols, the Fill button will be a chart of just coloured squares and the Mark & Fill button will be both of these things combined with symbols over a coloured square.

I've set this design to fit to one page because it's only a small design, but you could set that

to whatever you want so a larger design would print over multiple pages.

And we need to know what colours were used in the design, so you need to click on the Colour List button.

You can see here how the design would output containing all the information you need to sew the design.

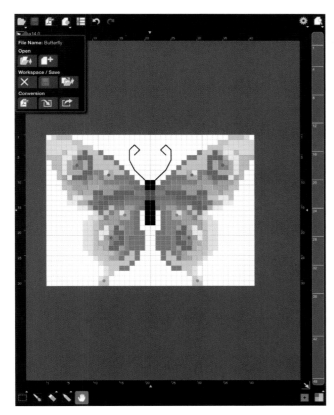

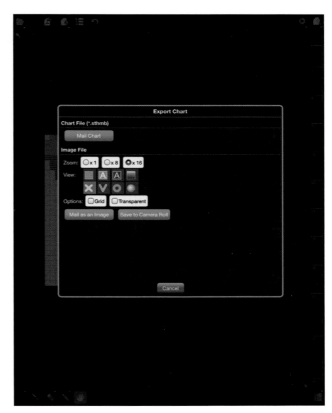

The app however doesn't attach a cover sheet to your chart with how the design would look sewn, so if you wanted to output that you would need to do it separately.

You can do this by clicking on the folder icon at the top left of the screen and then click on the icon at the very bottom right that resembles and arrow going out of a box.

This will bring up the export chart dialogue box, which allows you to export the chart as a .PNG file but it won't include the extra information about the chart such as the colour list as the PDF does.

If you click on the X button and leave off the grid then you can either mail the picture or simply save it to your camera roll.

This produces the chart made up of little x's in the correct colour and is the stitched simulation for this app.

Whilst it isn't as advanced as simulations from desktop software, it can be useful to let you see what the design is quickly, and is especially useful if you output your designs as black and white charts.

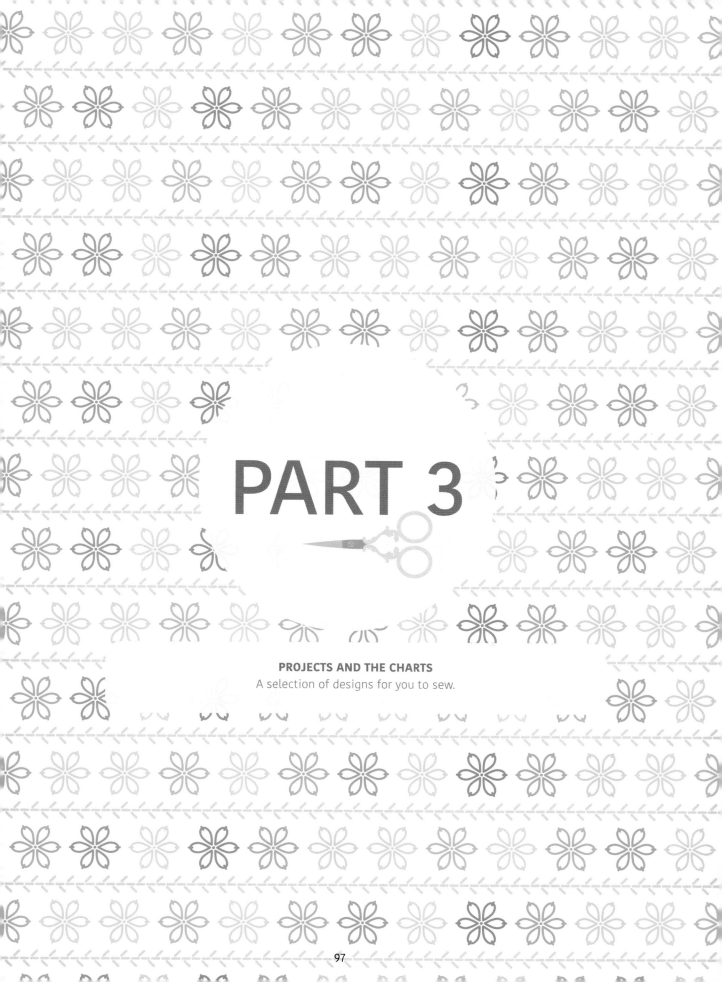

PART 3

PROJECTS AND THE CHARTS
A selection of designs for you to sew.

1 Chart on P.124

99

3 Chart on P.130

4 Chart on P.132

5 Chart on P.132

6 Chart on P.132

7 Chart on P.133

8 Chart on P.133

9 Chart on P.134

11 Chart on P.136

12 Chart on P.137

104

10 Chart on P.136

13 Chart on P.137

16 Chart on P.140

17 Chart on P.141

18 Chart on P.141

109

20 Chart on P.143

Spring
Flowers
Bringing life back

SPRING IS IN BLOOM
Dancing with flowers and singing with birds
Joy and happiness

21 Chart on P.143

22 Chart on P.143

30 Chart on P.159

31 Chart on P.159

32 Chart on P.159

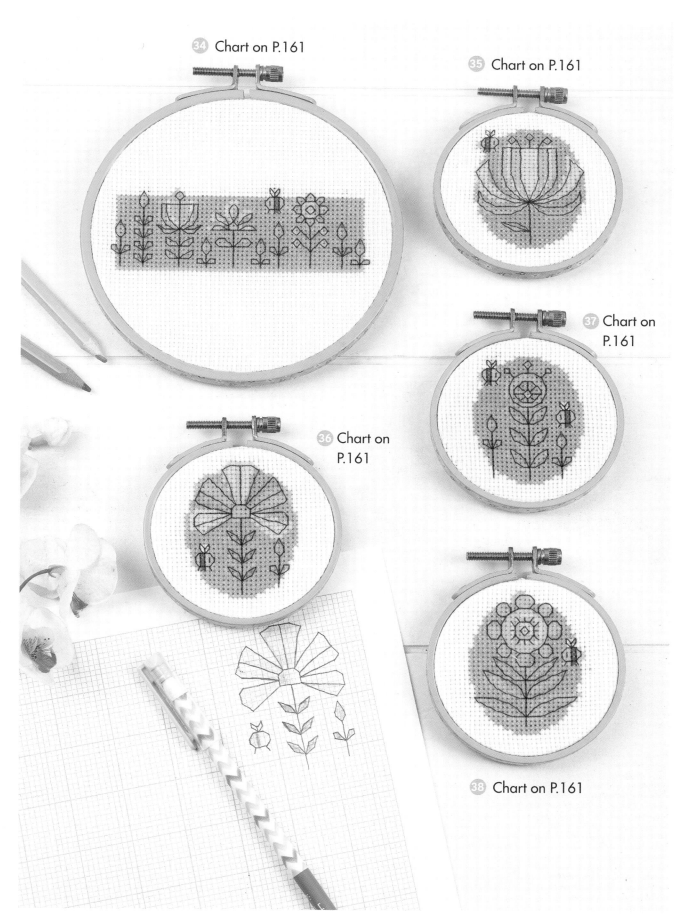

34 Chart on P.161

35 Chart on P.161

37 Chart on P.161

36 Chart on P.161

38 Chart on P.161

CHARTS

1

❶ Photo on P.98

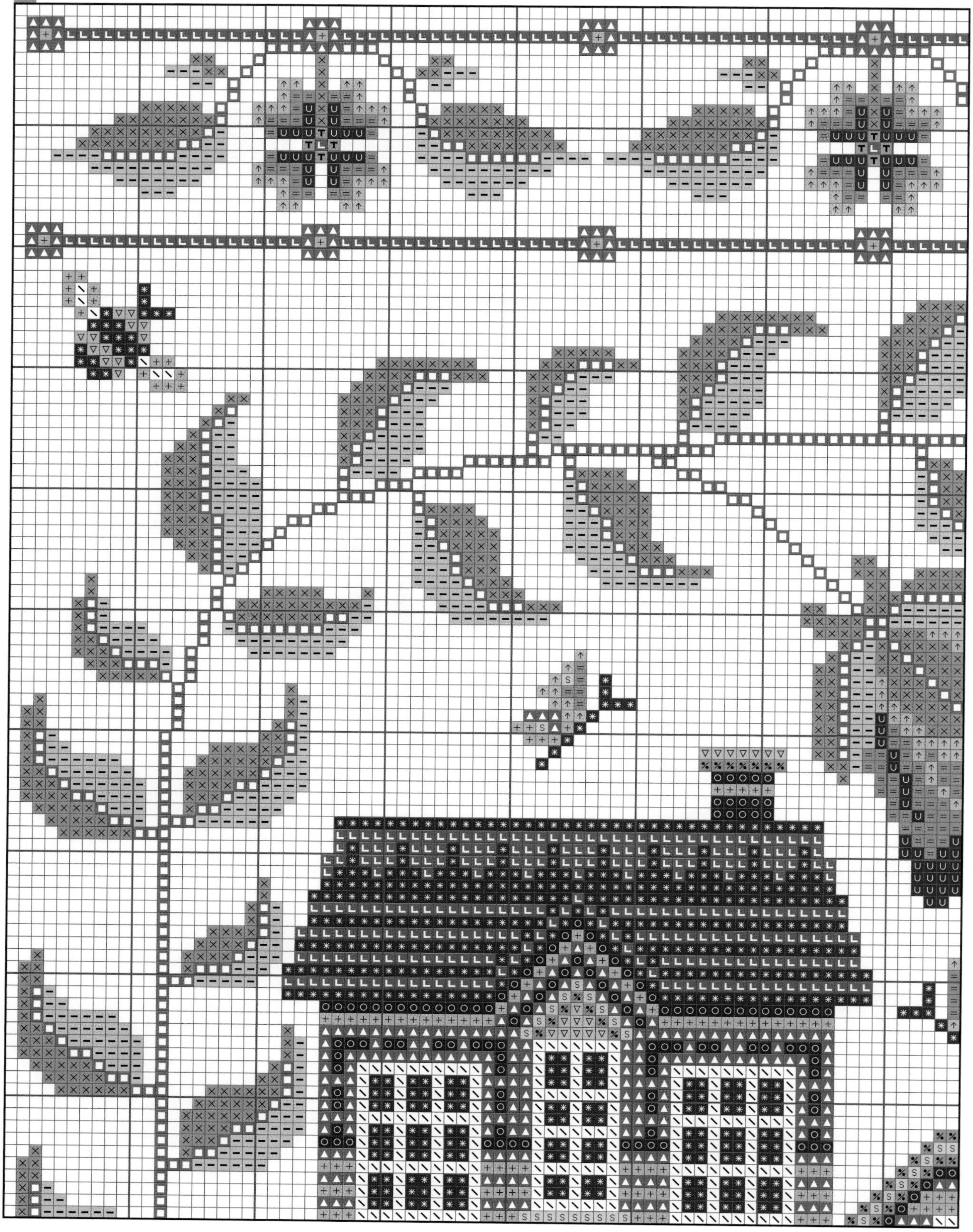

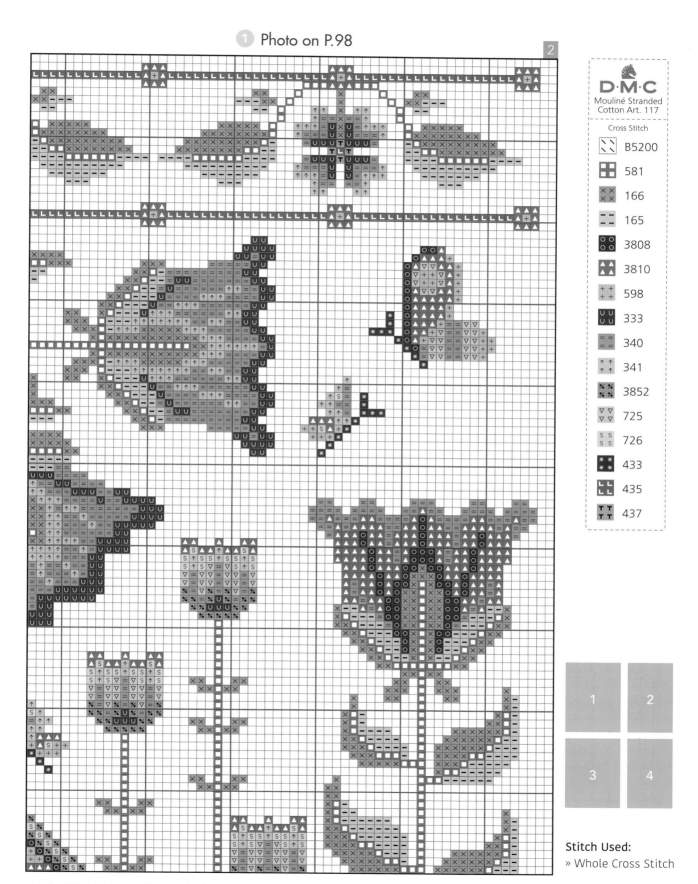

Cross Stitch	
◥◣	B5200
⊞	581
× ×	166
– –	165
○ ○	3808
▲ ▲	3810
+ +	598
U U	333
= =	340
↑ ↑	341
✹ ✹	3852
▽ ▽	725
S S	726
✱ ✱	433
L L	435
T T	437

DMC
Mouliné Stranded
Cotton Art. 117

Stitch Used:
» Whole Cross Stitch

Fabric: DMC 16ct Aida (DM842/712)
Design Size: 21 x 30cm

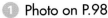

1 Photo on P.98

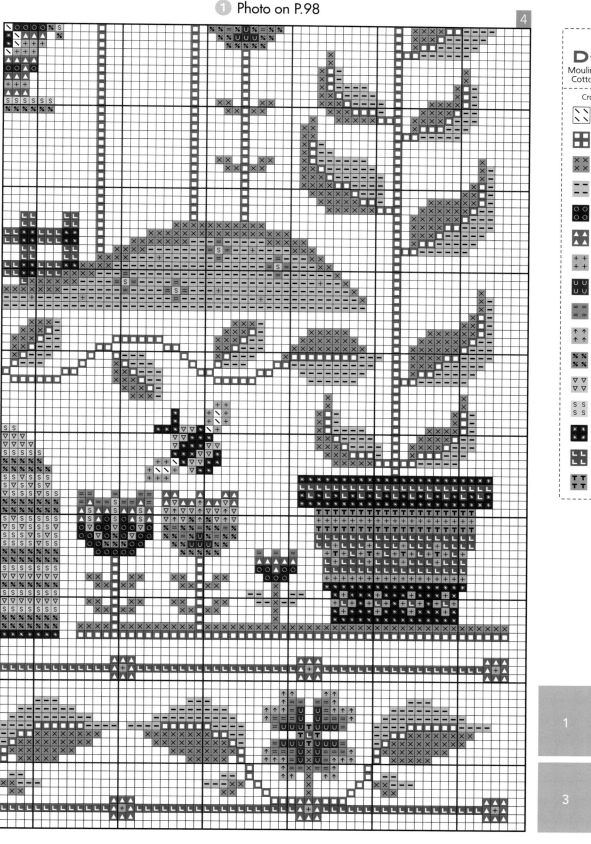

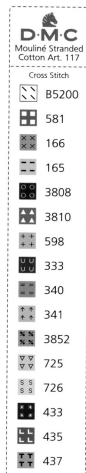

DMC
Mouliné Stranded
Cotton Art. 117

Cross Stitch

\\	B5200
⊞	581
✕	166
– –	165
○ ○	3808
▲▲	3810
+ +	598
U U	333
= =	340
↑ ↑	341
✕ ✕	3852
▽ ▽	725
S S	726
✱ ✱	433
L L	435
T T	437

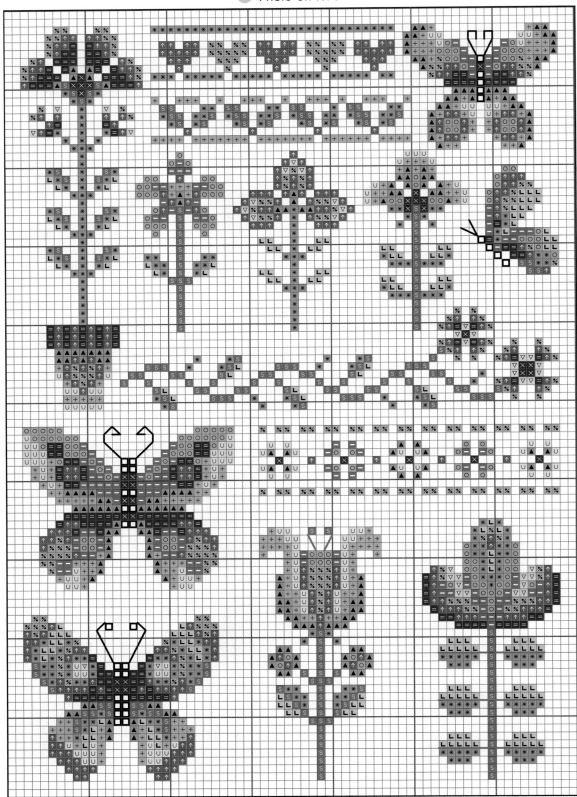

Fabric: DMC 16ct Aida (DM222/Blanc)
Design Size: 25 x 18cm

Themed Charts can be sewn individually or
used to make your own sampler as described
earlier in the book.

Stitch Used:
» Whole Cross Stitch
» Back Stitch

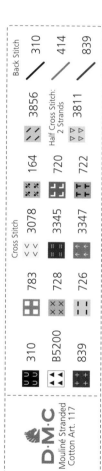

Fabric: DMC 16ct Aida (DM842/Blanc)
Design Size: 15 x 21cm

Stitch Used:
» Whole Cross Stitch
» Half Cross Stitch
» Back Stitch

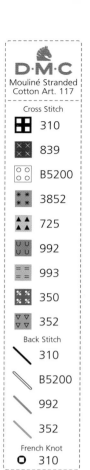

DMC

Mouliné Stranded
Cotton Art. 117

Cross Stitch

⊞	310
××	839
∘∘	B5200
**	3852
▲▲	725
UU	992
==	993
××	350
▽▽	352

Back Stitch

╲	310
╱	B5200
╱	992
╱	352

French Knot

O	310

④ **Photo on P.101**

Stitch Used:
» Whole Cross Stitch » Fractional Stitches » Back Stitch » French Knot
Fabric: DMC 14ct Aida (DM222/Blanc) / **Design Size:** 13 x 9cm

⑤ **Photo on P.101**

⑥ **Photo on P.101**

Stitch Used:
» Whole Cross Stitch
» Diagonal Fractional Stitch
» Squashed Fractional Stitch
» Straddled Cross Stitch
» Back Stitch
» Lazy Daisy

Fabric: DMC 14ct Aida (DM222/Blanc)
Design Size: 6 x 9cm

Fabric: DMC 14ct Aida (DM222/Blanc)
Design Size: 6 x 9cm

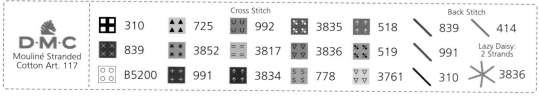

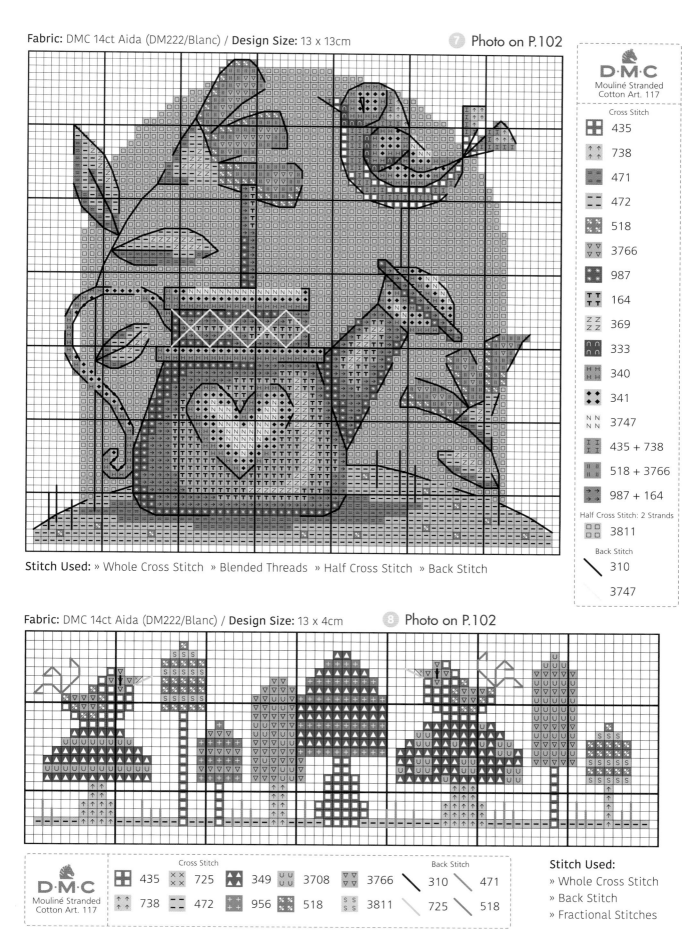

D·M·C
Mouliné Stranded
Cotton Art. 117

Cross Stitch

⊞	435
↑↑	738
==	471
--	472
✕✕	518
▽▽	3766
✳✳	987
T T	164
Z Z	369
∩∩	333
H H	340
◆◆	341
N N	3747
I I	435 + 738
‖‖	518 + 3766
→→	987 + 164

Half Cross Stitch: 2 Strands

☐☐	3811

Back Stitch

╲	310
	3747

Stitch Used: » Whole Cross Stitch » Blended Threads » Half Cross Stitch » Back Stitch

D·M·C
Mouliné Stranded
Cotton Art. 117

Cross Stitch

⊞ 435	✕✕ 725	▲ 349	UU 3708	▽▽ 3766	Back Stitch ╲ 310	╲ 471
↑↑ 738	-- 472	++ 956	✕✕ 518	SS 3811	╲ 725	╲ 518

Stitch Used:
» Whole Cross Stitch
» Back Stitch
» Fractional Stitches

SAMANTHA JE

24.10.21

D·M·C

Mouliné Stranded
Cotton Art. 117

Cross Stitch

oo	603
▲▲	605
++	818
==	743
↑↑	744
%%	745
▽▽	911
ss	913
**	955
TT	809
\\	800
<<	162
→→	436
II	738
ZZ	739

Mill Hill Seed Bead

××	00525
UU	02002

Back Stitch: 1 Strand

\ 3799

Back Stitch: 2 Strands

\ 436

French Knot

● 436

Stitch Used:
» Whole Cross Stitch
» Back Stitch
» French Knot
» Bead

Fabric: DMC 14ct Aida (DM222/Blanc)
Design Size: 25 x 18cm

DMC
Mouliné Stranded
Cotton Art. 117

Cross Stitch

209	
210	
211	
581	
166	
3819	
970	
741	
742	
739	
798	
809	
800	

Back Stitch

310

Mill Hill Seed Bead

02085

6mm orange sequin attached using a seed bead

Stitch Used:

» Whole Cross Stitch » Back Stitch » Bead » Sequin

Fabric: DMC 28ct Evenweave (DM542A/Blanc)
Design Size: 13 x 13cm

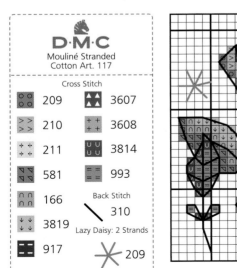

DMC
Mouliné Stranded
Cotton Art. 117

Cross Stitch

209		3607	
210		3608	
211		3814	
581		993	
166		**Back Stitch**	
3819		310	
917		**Lazy Daisy: 2 Strands**	
		209	

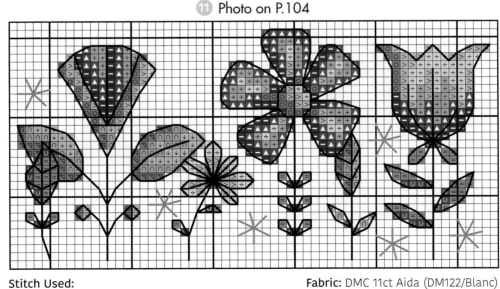

Stitch Used:

» Whole Cross Stitch » Back Stitch » Lazy Daisy

Fabric: DMC 11ct Aida (DM122/Blanc)
Design Size: 13 x 7cm

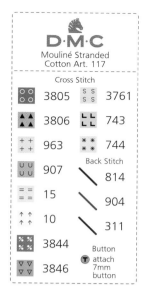

D·M·C
Mouliné Stranded
Cotton Art. 117

Cross Stitch

○○	3805	SS	3761
▲▲	3806	LL	743
++	963	**	744
UU	907		
==	15		
↑↑	10		
✗✗	3844		
▽▽	3846		

Back Stitch

╲ 814
╲ 904
╲ 311

Button
Ⓣ attach 7mm button

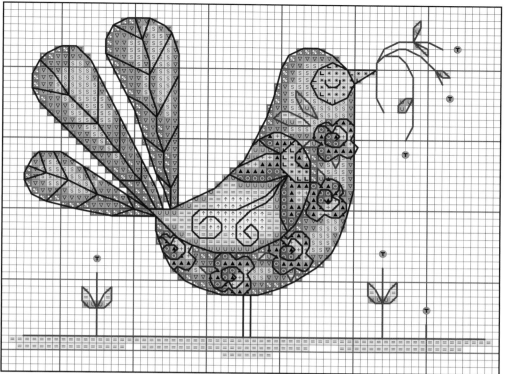

Stitch Used:
» Whole Cross Stitch
» Back Stitch
» Attached Buttons

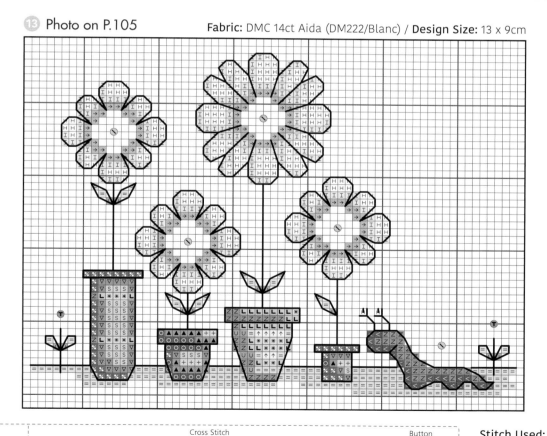

D·M·C
Mouliné Stranded
Cotton Art. 117

Cross Stitch

→→	415	○○	3805	UU	907	✗✗	3844	LL	743
II	762	▲▲	3806	==	15	▽▽	3846	**	744
HH	B5200	++	963	↑↑	10	SS	3761	<<	420

ZZ 422

Button
Ⓣ attach 7mm button
Ⓝ attach 10mm button

Back Stitch
╲ 310

Stitch Used:
» Whole Cross Stitch
» Back Stitch
» Attached Buttons

	DMC
	Mouliné Stranded Cotton Art. 117

Cross Stitch

	163
⌀⌀	3816
SS / SS	3817
	3847
NN / NN	3849
44 / 44	964
	826
UU / UU	813
↑↑ / ↑↑	827
++ / ++	162
⠒	B5200
⊏⊏	E747
◦◦ / ◦◦	E5200

Half Cross Stitch: 1 Strand

** / **	3811

Back Stitch

╲	823

Stitch Used:

» Whole Cross Stitch

» Half Cross Stitch

» Back Stitch

» Metalic Threads

Fabric: DMC 14ct Aida (DM222/Blanc)

Design Size: 13 x 19cm

Cross Stitch	
434	
436	
437	
739	
712	
702	
704	
3346	
989	
164	
369	
772	
972	
726	
727	
815	
349	
351	
3325	
775	

Back Stitch
3346
815
351
434

French Knot
351
727

Fabric: DMC 18ct Aida (DM322/712)
Design Size: 10 x 14cm

Stitch Used:
» Whole Cross Stitch
» Back Stitch
» French Knot

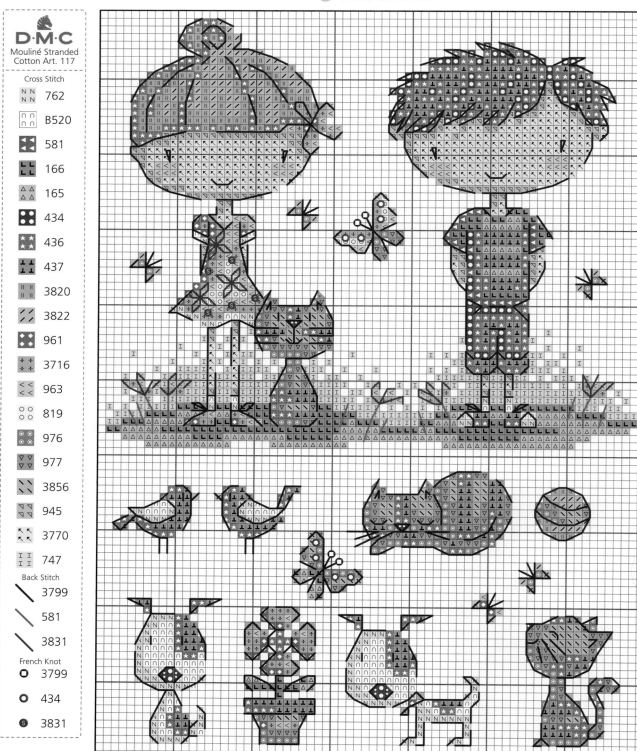

D·M·C
Mouliné Stranded
Cotton Art. 117

Cross Stitch

N N / N N	762
∩ ∩ / ∩ ∩	B520
	581
L L / L L	166
△ △ / △ △	165
	434
★ ★ / ★ ★	436
⊥ ⊥ / ⊥ ⊥	437
‖ ‖ / ‖ ‖	3820
∕ ∕ / ∕ ∕	3822
	961
‡ ‡ / ‡ ‡	3716
< < / < <	963
○ ○ / ○ ○	819
◉ ◉ / ◉ ◉	976
▽ ▽ / ▽ ▽	977
＼ ＼ / ＼ ＼	3856
◁ ◁ / ◁ ◁	945
↖ ↖ / ↖ ↖	3770
I I / I I	747

Back Stitch

＼	3799
╱	581
＼	3831

French Knot

O	3799
o	434
S	3831

Mix and Match Charts

Use the small elements to practice personalising
the main charts.

Fabric: DMC 14ct Aida (DM222/Blanc)
Design Size: 13 x 19cm

Stitch Used:
» Whole Cross Stitch
» Fractional Stitches
» Back Stitch
» French Knot

Fabric: Zweigart 20ct Bellana (DM3256/100)
Design Size: 17 x 15cm

17 Photo on P.109

Fabric: DMC 11ct Aida (DM122/Blanc)
Design Size: 15 x 9cm

18 Photo on P.109

D·M·C
Mouliné Stranded
Cotton Art. 117

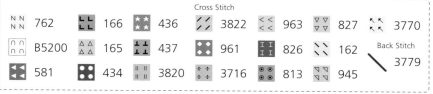

						Cross Stitch						
NN NN	762	LL LL	166	★★ ★★	436	╱╱ ╱╱	3822	<< <<	963	▽▽ ▽▽	827	⤢⤢ 3770
∩∩ ∩∩	B5200	△△ △△	165	⊥⊥ ⊥⊥	437	◈◈	961	II II	826	╲╲	162	Back Stitch
❖❖	581	❖❖	434	‖‖	3820	╬╬	3716	◉◉	813	▽▽	945	3779

Stitch Used:
» Whole Cross Stitch
» Back Stitch

Fabric: DMC 16ct Aida (DM842/Blanc)
Design Size: 11 x 15cm

19 Photo on P.110

Stitch Used:

» Whole Cross Stitch
» Back Stitch
» French Knot

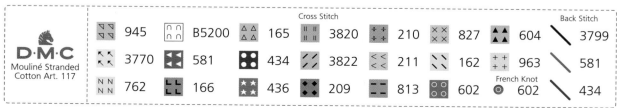

						Cross Stitch											Back Stitch	
945		B5200		165		3820		210		827		604				3799
3770		581		434		3822		211		162		963				581
762		166		436		209		813		602		French Knot 602				434

DMC
Mouliné Stranded
Cotton Art. 117

Fabric: DMC 14ct Aida (DM222/712)
Design Size: 9 x 9cm

⓴ Photo on P.111

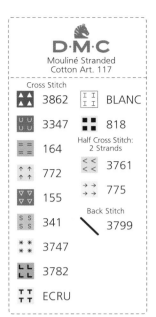

Cross Stitch		
3862	3347	164
BLANC	818	

DMC
Mouliné Stranded
Cotton Art. 117

Cross Stitch

▲▲	3862		I I	BLANC
UU	3347		■ ■	818
= =	164	Half Cross Stitch: 2 Strands		
↑↑	772		< <	3761
▽▽	155		→ →	775
S S	341	Back Stitch		
✱✱	3747		╲	3799
L L	3782			
T T	ECRU			

Stitch Used:
» Whole Cross Stitch
» Half Cross Stitch
» Back Stitch

㉑ Photo on P.111

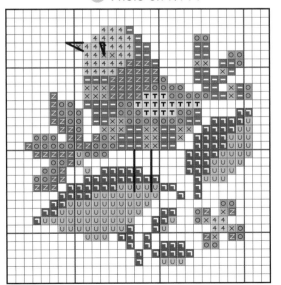

Fabric: DMC 14ct Aida (DM222/Blanc)
Design Size: 6 x 6cm

㉒ Photo on P.111

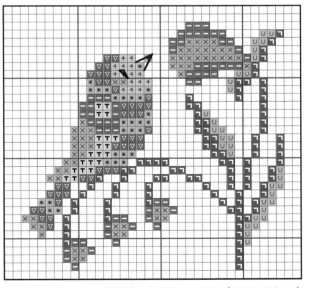

Fabric: DMC 14ct Aida (DM222/Blanc)
Design Size: 5 x 5cm

Stitch Used:
» Whole Cross Stitch
» Back Stitch

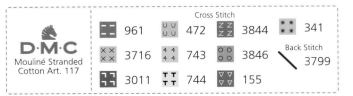

DMC
Mouliné Stranded
Cotton Art. 117

Cross Stitch							
■	961	U U	472	Z Z	3844	✱✱	341
✕✕	3716	4 4	743	○○	3846	Back Stitch	3799
■	3011	T T	744	▽▽	155		

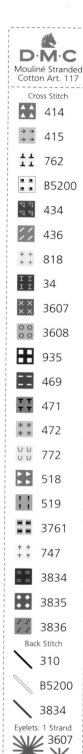

Fabric: DMC 28ct Evenweave (DM542A/Blanc)
Design Size: 25 x 17cm

Stitch Used:
» Whole Cross Stitch
» Back Stitch
» Eyelets

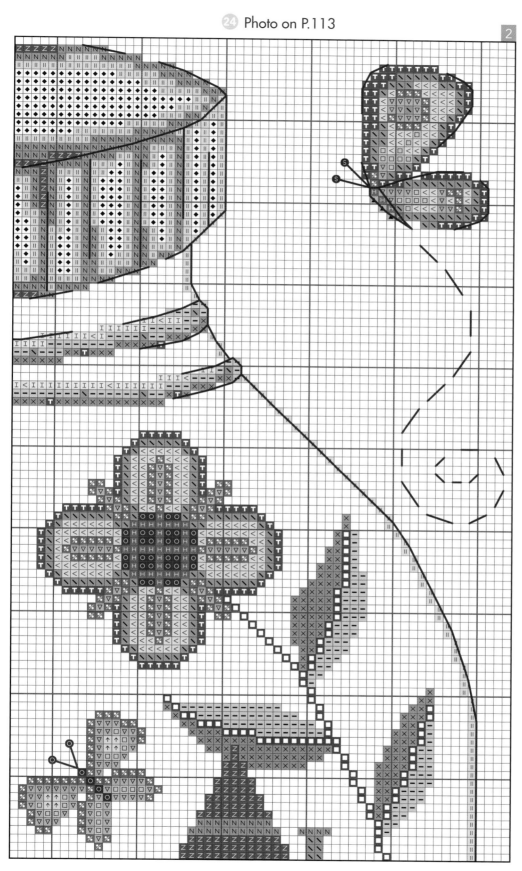

DMC
Mouliné Stranded Cotton Art. 117

Cross Stitch
Z Z	3809
N N	597
II II	3811
○○	433
H H	435
▲▲	437
◆◆	712
⊞	937
✕✕	471
▬	3348
I I	772
⁏⁏	720
▽▽	722
□□	3856
T T	3350
◥◥	3733
<<	151
∩∩	725
↑↑	726

Back Stitch
╲	3799
╱	433
╱	720

French Knot
●	3799
⊙	433

1 2
3 4

Stitch Used:
» Whole Cross Stitch » Back Stitch » French Knot

Fabric: DMC 18ct Aida (DM322/Blanc)
Design Size: 19 x 27cm

3

24 Photo on P.113

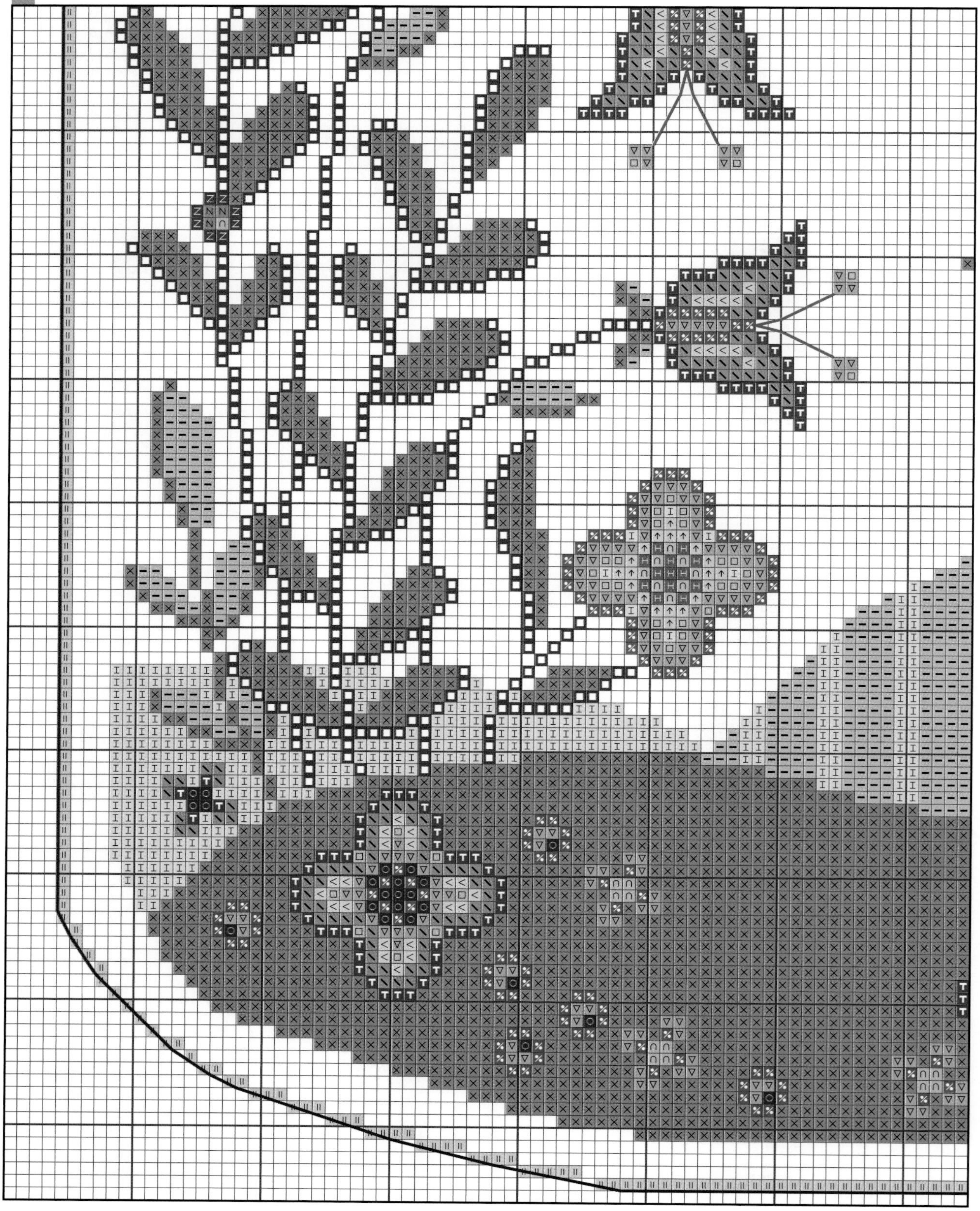

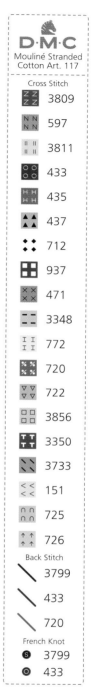

DMC
Mouliné Stranded
Cotton Art. 117

Cross Stitch

Z Z / Z Z	3809
N N / N N	597
II II / II II	3811
oo / oo	433
H H / H H	435
▲▲ / ▲▲	437
◆◆ / ◆◆	712
⊞	937
×× / ××	471
-- / --	3348
I I / I I	772
⁕⁕ / ⁕⁕	720
▽▽ / ▽▽	722
□□ / □□	3856
T T / T T	3350
＼＼ / ＼＼	3733
<< / <<	151
∩∩ / ∩∩	725
↑↑ / ↑↑	726

Back Stitch

＼	3799
╱	433
＼	720

French Knot

⬤	3799
◎	433

1	2
3	4

149

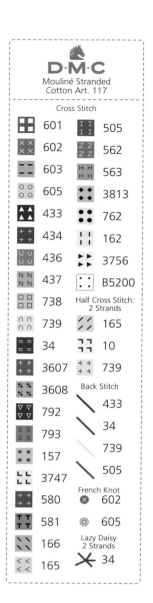

DMC
Mouliné Stranded
Cotton Art. 117

Cross Stitch

601		505	
602		562	
603		563	
605		3813	
433		762	
434		162	
436		3756	
437		B5200	
738			

Half Cross Stitch: 2 Strands

739		165	
34		10	
3607		739	

3608		Back Stitch
792		433
793		34
157		739
3747		505

French Knot

580		602
581		605

166		Lazy Daisy 2 Strands
165		34

Stitch Used:
» Whole Cross Stitch
» Half Cross Stitch
» Back Stitch
» French Knot
» Lazy Daisy

Fabric: DMC 16ct Aida (DM842/Blanc)
Design Size: 31 x 15cm

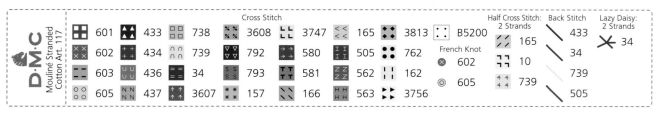

Fabric: DMC 14ct Aida (DM222/Blanc)
Design Size: 13 x 19cm

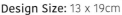 **26 Photo on P.115**

D·M·C
Mouliné Stranded
Cotton Art. 117

	Cross Stitch			Back Stitch	Double Cross Stitch: 2 Strands Coloris Thread

Stitch Used:
» Whole Cross Stitch
» Double Cross Stitch
» Back Stitch
» French Knot

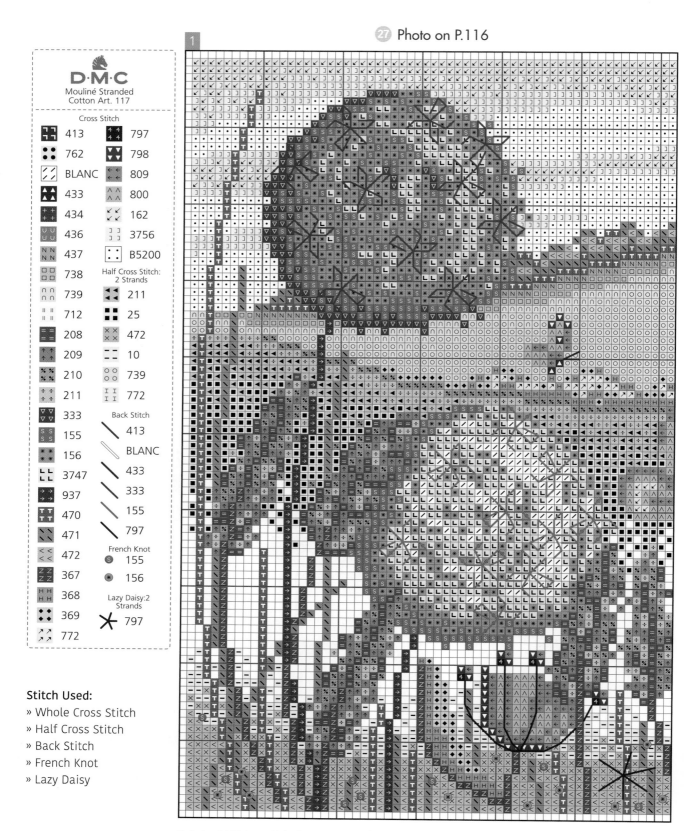

D·M·C
Mouliné Stranded
Cotton Art. 117

Cross Stitch

413		797		
762		798		
BLANC		809		
433		800		
434		162		
436		3756		
437		B5200		
738				

Half Cross Stitch: 2 Strands

739		211		
712		25		
208		472		
209		10		
210		739		
211		772		

333

Back Stitch

155 — 413
156 — BLANC
3747 — 433
937 — 333
470 — 155
471 — 797

French Knot
472 — 155
367 — 156

Lazy Daisy: 2 Strands
368
369 — 797
772

Stitch Used:

» Whole Cross Stitch
» Half Cross Stitch
» Back Stitch
» French Knot
» Lazy Daisy

Fabric: DMC 16ct Aida (DM842/Blanc)
Design Size: 31 x 15cm

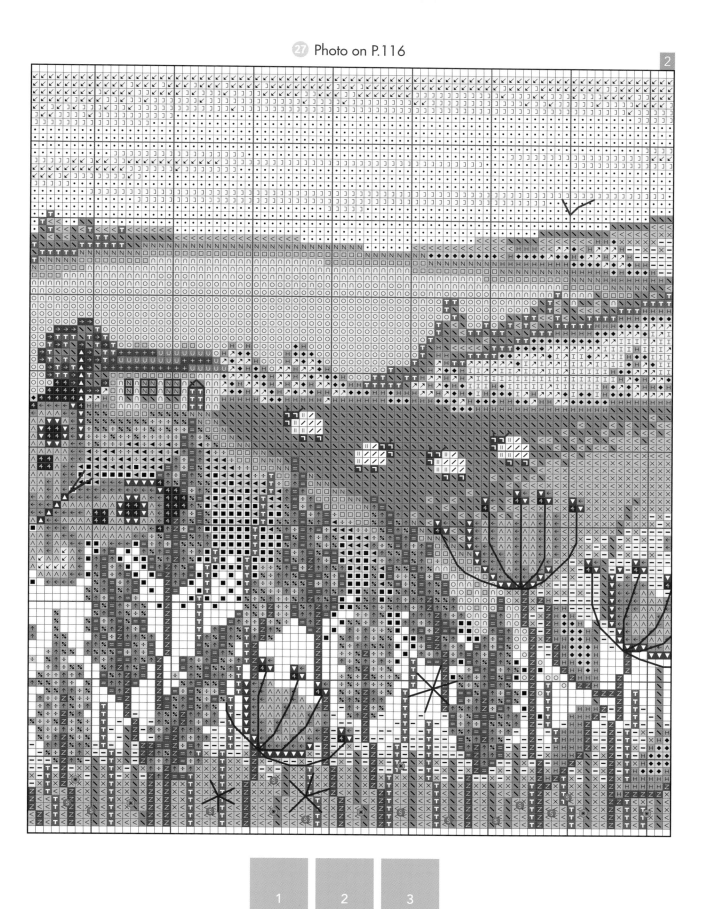

D·M·C
Mouliné Stranded
Cotton Art. 117

Cross Stitch

413		797	
762		798	
BLANC		809	
433		800	
434		162	
436		3756	
437		B5200	
738			
739		**Half Cross Stitch:** 2 Strands	
712		211	
208		25	
209		472	
210		10	
211		739	
333		772	
155			
156		**Back Stitch**	
3747		413	
937		BLANC	
470		433	
471		333	
472		155	
367		797	
368			
369		**French Knot**	
772		155	
		156	

Lazy Daisy: 2 Strands
797

1   2   3

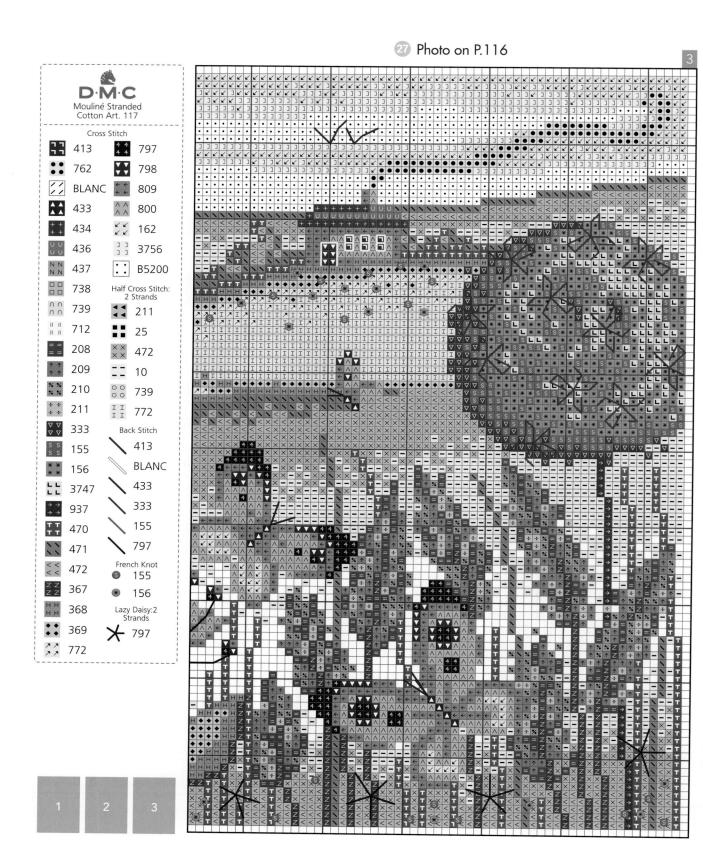

Fabric: DMC 16ct Aida (DM842/Blanc)
Design Size: 11 x 15cm

28 Photo on P.117

Stitch Used:
» Whole Cross Stitch
» Half Cross Stitch
» Back Stitch
» Lazy Daisy

DMC Mouliné Stranded Cotton Art. 117	Cross Stitch					Half Cross Stitch: 2 Strands	Back Stitch	Lazy Daisy: 2 Strands
	310	976	722	166	3705	818	827	3708
	975	977	3856	165	3708		310	
	3826	721	906	10	605	162	975	3705

157

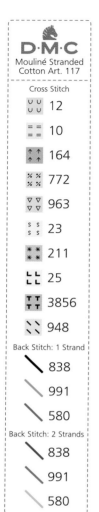

Stitch Used:
» Whole Cross Stitch
» Back Stitch

Fabric: DMC 14ct Aida (DM222/Blanc)
Design Size: 12 x 19cm

Themed Set could be used to practice putting together multiple designs into one design as described in the text.

Also contains more advanced back stitch techniques using back stitch in one and two strands and in multiple colours.

Fabric: DMC 28ct Evenweave (DM542A/Blanc)
Design Size: 9 x 10cm

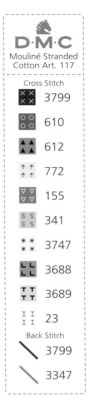

30 Photo on P.119

D·M·C
Mouliné Stranded
Cotton Art. 117

Cross Stitch

✗✗	3799
○○	610
▲▲	612
↑↑	772
▽▽	155
ss	341
✳✳	3747
LL	3688
TT	3689
II	23

Back Stitch

╱	3799
╱	3347

Stitch Used:
» Whole Cross Stitch
» Back Stitch
» Petit Point - 1 Strand

---

31 Photo on P.119

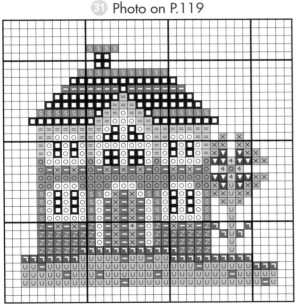

Fabric: DMC 14ct Aida (DM222/Blanc)
Design Size: 6 x 6cm

---

32 Photo on P.119

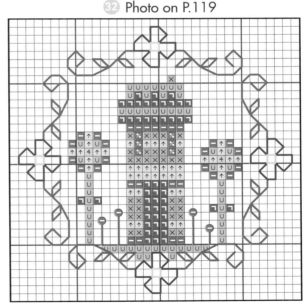

Fabric: DMC 11ct Aida (DM124/Blanc)
Design Size: 8 x 8cm

Stitch Used:
» Whole Cross Stitch
» Blended Threads
» Back Stitch
» French Knot

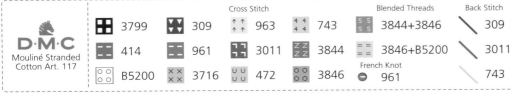

D·M·C
Mouliné Stranded
Cotton Art. 117

Cross Stitch				Blended Threads	Back Stitch	
▦ 3799	▼ 309	↑↑ 963	⁴⁴ 743	ss 3844+3846	╱ 309	
▤ 414	▤ 961	▦ 3011	zz 3844	== 3846+B5200	╱ 3011	
○○ B5200	✗✗ 3716	UU 472	○○ 3846	French Knot ● 961	╱ 743	

159

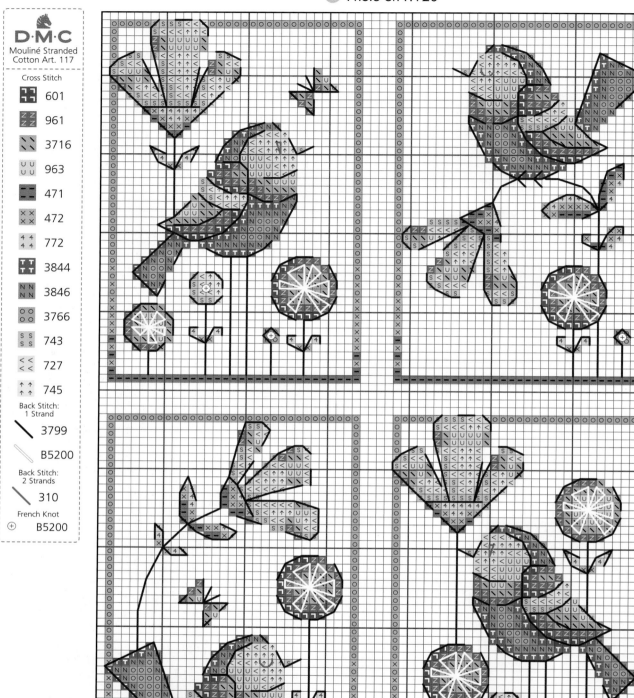

D·M·C
Mouliné Stranded
Cotton Art. 117

Cross Stitch

ᄀ	601
Z Z	961
\ \	3716
U U	963
– –	471
X X	472
4 4	772
T T	3844
N N	3846
o o	3766
S S	743
< <	727
↑ ↑	745

Back Stitch:
1 Strand
／ 3799
／ B5200

Back Stitch:
2 Strands
／ 310

French Knot
⊕ B5200

Themed Set
Could be used to practice putting together multiple designs into one design as described in the text.

Stitch Used:
» Whole Cross Stitch
» Back Stitch
» French Knot

Fabric: DMC 14ct Aida (DM222/Blanc)
Design Size: 13 x 18cm

Fabric: DMC 14ct Aida (DM222/Blanc)
Design Size: 11 x 4cm

34 Photo on P.121

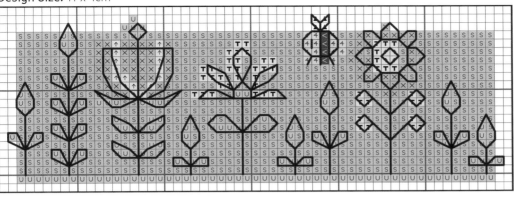

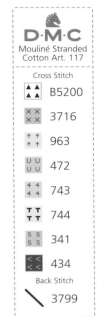

DMC
Mouliné Stranded
Cotton Art. 117

Cross Stitch

▲▲ ▲▲	B5200
×× ××	3716
↑↑ ↑↑	963
UU UU	472
44 44	743
TT TT	744
SS SS	341
<< <<	434

Back Stitch

| ╱ | 3799 |

Stitch Used:
» Whole Cross Stitch
» Back Stitch

35 Photo on P.121

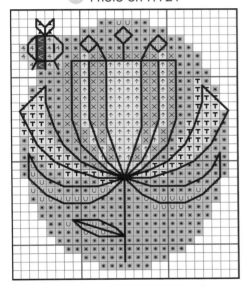

Fabric: DMC 14ct Aida (DM222/Blanc)
Design Size: 5 x 6cm

36 Photo on P.121

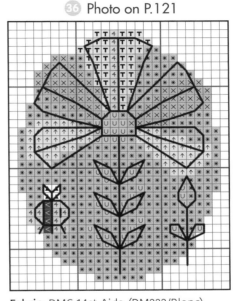

Fabric: DMC 14ct Aida (DM222/Blanc)
Design Size: 5 x 6cm

37 Photo on P.121

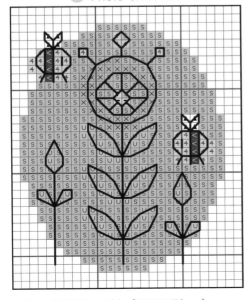

Fabric: DMC 14ct Aida (DM222/Blanc)
Design Size: 5 x 6cm

38 Photo on P.121

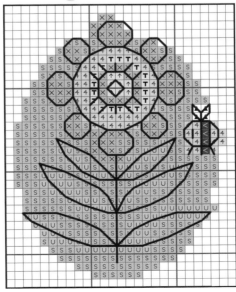

Fabric: DMC 14ct Aida (DM222/Blanc)
Design Size: 5 x 6cm

Stitch Used:

» Whole Cross Stitch

» Back Stitch

» Lazy Daisy

Fabric: Zweigart 28ct Cashel (3281/100)

Design Size: 17 x 24cm

Cross Stitch		
310	3608	739
34	435	472
3607	437	469
		471
		519
		517
		518
		3836
		3834

Back Stitch

/ 310

/ 469

Lazy Daisy: 2 Strands

✕ 3835

/ 3835

D·M·C
Mouliné Stranded
Cotton Art. 117

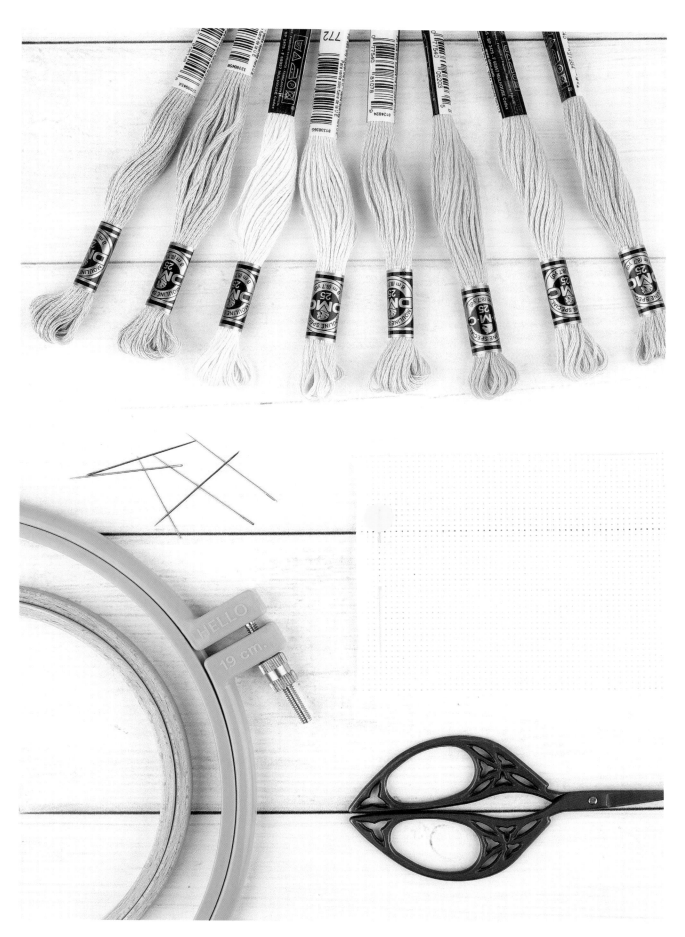